Motivational Inte
Neurodiverge

Evidence-Based Techniques for ADHD, Autism,
and Executive Function Support

Robin Sable Blume

First Edition

ISBN (Paperback): 978-1-923604-00-1

ISBN (eBook): 978-1-923604-01-8

This book is for educational and informational purposes only. The content is not intended to be a substitute for professional medical advice, diagnosis, or treatment. Always seek the advice of qualified mental health professionals with any questions you may have regarding therapeutic interventions or neurodivergent conditions.

All names used throughout this book are fictional. Client names including Alex, Emma, Sarah, Marcus, David, Jessica, Jake, Lisa, Michael, Hannah, Jason, Maya, Kevin, Maria, Rachel, Ben, Jennifer, Jordan, Kai, Lily, Tom, and Mike are entirely fictitious. Professional names including Dr. Martinez, Dr. Chen, Dr. Rodriguez, Dr. Kumar, Dr. Park, Dr. Rivera, Dr. Thompson, Dr. Williams, and Dr. Patterson are also fictional. Any resemblance to actual persons, living or dead, is purely coincidental. Case examples are composites based on clinical patterns and experiences rather than specific individuals.

The author and publisher disclaim any liability arising directly or indirectly from the use of this book.

Table of Contents

Preface

When I first encountered motivational interviewing in graduate school, I was struck by its elegance and effectiveness. The collaborative spirit, the respect for individual autonomy, and the skillful way it helped people find their own motivation for change felt revolutionary compared to more directive therapeutic approaches I had learned.

But as I began working with neurodivergent clients—individuals with autism, ADHD, and other neurological differences—I noticed something troubling. The same techniques that worked beautifully with neurotypical clients often fell flat or even backfired with neurodivergent individuals. Open-ended questions created confusion rather than exploration. Reflective listening felt patronizing rather than validating. Traditional therapeutic environments seemed to drain rather than energize my neurodivergent clients.

I realized that motivational interviewing, despite its person-centered philosophy, was built on neurotypical assumptions about communication, social interaction, sensory processing, and motivation. These assumptions weren't intentionally exclusionary, but they created significant barriers for people whose brains worked differently.

This book represents over Ten years of learning, adapting, and discovering how to make motivational interviewing truly accessible to neurodivergent individuals. It's not about abandoning MI principles—it's about honoring those principles while adapting the methods to work with different neurological realities.

Throughout this book, I use detailed case examples to illustrate concepts and techniques. All names and identifying details are fictional, created specifically for this book to protect client confidentiality while providing realistic, representative scenarios.

Alex, Emma, Sarah, Marcus, David, Jessica, Jake, Lisa, Michael, Hannah, Jason, Maya, Kevin, Maria, Rachel, Ben, Jennifer, Jordan, Kai, Lily, Tom, Mike, and others represent the range of ages, backgrounds, and experiences within neurodivergent communities. I selected names that are common across different cultural backgrounds to reflect the reality that neurodivergence occurs across all demographics.

Professional names used in this book (e.g., Dr. Martinez, Dr. Chen, Dr. Rodriguez, Dr. Kumar, Dr. Park, Dr. Rivera, Dr. Thompson, Dr. Williams, Dr. Patterson) are fictitious and created solely for this work. They stand in for the many clinicians, educators, and other professionals learning to adapt their practice for neurodivergent individuals. Any resemblance to actual persons is coincidental.

Each case example is a composite drawn from clinical experience, consultation work, and the generous sharing of neurodivergent individuals who have taught me what works and what doesn't in therapeutic settings. While no single case represents a real person, each reflects genuine patterns and experiences I've encountered in my work.

This work has been deeply influenced by the neurodivergent individuals who have shared their experiences, insights, and feedback with me over the years. Their willingness to explain what works and what doesn't, to tolerate my mistakes as I learned, and to celebrate successes together has made this book possible.

I also want to acknowledge the growing community of neurodivergent professionals who are transforming fields like psychology, education, and social work from the inside. Their perspectives challenge assumptions that the rest of us might never have questioned and create more inclusive approaches that benefit everyone.

Finally, I recognize that this book represents one step in an ongoing journey. Our understanding of neurodivergence continues to evolve, and the voices of neurodivergent individuals themselves must remain central to that evolution. I hope this book serves as a bridge—making motivational interviewing more accessible while supporting the broader movement toward truly neurodiversity-affirming practices.

The goal isn't to make neurodivergent people more neurotypical. It's to create therapeutic approaches that honor and work with the beautiful diversity of human brains, helping everyone access their motivation for positive change in ways that feel authentic and sustainable.

This book is written for anyone who believes that different brains deserve approaches that work with their strengths rather than against their nature. Whether you're a mental health professional, educator, parent, or neurodivergent individual seeking better therapeutic experiences, I hope you'll find practical tools and perspectives that make meaningful change more possible.

Robin Sable Blume

Chapter 1: Different Brains, Different Conversations

Neurological considerations

Sarah sits across from her therapist, fidgeting with a small rubber cube in her hands. The therapist leans forward with what she hopes is an encouraging smile and asks, "What would you like to be different in your life?" Sarah's eyes dart to the window, then to her hands, anywhere but the therapist's face. After a long pause, she responds with laser precision: "Different how? Different from what baseline? Are we talking about behavioral changes, environmental modifications, or internal state alterations?"

The therapist blinks. She wasn't expecting a request for clarification of her open-ended question. This is motivational interviewing 101—start broad, let the client guide the conversation. But Sarah's brain doesn't work the way the textbooks assume brains work.

Welcome to the reality of motivational interviewing with neurodivergent minds.

Understanding neurodivergent brain differences

Traditional motivational interviewing assumes certain things about how brains process information, handle social interaction, and respond to emotional appeals. These assumptions work beautifully for neurotypical individuals. For neurodivergent people—those with autism, ADHD, and other neurological differences—these same assumptions can create barriers instead of bridges to change.

Neurodivergent brains aren't broken versions of typical brains. They're different operating systems running on different hardware. When we try to run neurotypical software on neurodivergent hardware, things get glitchy fast.

4

The autism spectrum brings us minds that process information with remarkable precision but struggle with ambiguity. An autistic person might interpret "How are you feeling about this?" as genuinely requesting a detailed physiological and emotional status report rather than recognizing it as a conversation opener. Their brains excel at pattern recognition and systematic thinking but may miss the subtle social cues that guide typical therapeutic conversations.

ADHD brains operate on a different reward system entirely. The neurotypical assumption that people can sustain attention on important-but-boring topics falls apart when dopamine doesn't fire for "should" activities. An ADHD brain might fully engage with passionate intensity about topics that capture their interest while appearing distracted or resistant when discussing changes they intellectually know they need to make.

These aren't character flaws or deficits in willpower. They're neurological realities that require us to adapt our approach.

Dr. Ari Ne'eman, a prominent autism self-advocate, explains that autistic people often process social and emotional information differently, not deficiently (Ne'eman, 2010). When we understand these differences as variations rather than impairments, we can work with the brain's natural patterns instead of against them.

Research in neurodiversity reveals that executive function differences in ADHD aren't about lacking motivation—they're about having a brain that requires different kinds of scaffolding to support planning, attention, and follow-through (Barkley, 2018). The dopamine dysregulation that characterizes ADHD means that traditional motivational approaches that rely on delayed gratification or "should" motivation often fail to engage the brain's reward circuits.

Traditional MI assumptions vs. neurodivergent realities

Classic motivational interviewing rests on several foundational assumptions that don't always match neurodivergent cognitive patterns. Let's examine where these assumptions break down and why.

Assumption 1: Open-ended questions promote exploration

Traditional MI trains us to ask broad, exploratory questions like "Tell me about your concerns" or "What brings you here today?" The theory suggests that open-ended questions give people space to share what's most important to them.

Neurodivergent reality: Many autistic individuals find open-ended questions overwhelming or confusing. Without clear parameters, they may not know where to start or what level of detail is expected. An autistic person might respond to "Tell me about your concerns" with either a overwhelmed silence or an exhaustively detailed forty-minute monologue covering every possible interpretation of the word "concerns."

Better approach: Start with more structured questions that still honor the person's autonomy. "I'm curious about three specific areas of your life—work, relationships, and daily routines. Which of these would you like to talk about first?" This provides structure while preserving choice.

Assumption 2: Reflective listening builds rapport

Standard MI emphasizes reflecting back what you hear, often with slight emotional amplification: "It sounds like you're really frustrated with how things are going at work."

Neurodivergent reality: Some autistic individuals interpret reflective statements as the listener not paying attention or not understanding correctly. If they just explained their situation, why is the person repeating it back differently? This can feel condescending or confusing rather than validating.

ADHD individuals might find reflective listening slow and repetitive, causing their attention to drift just when you're trying to build connection.

Better approach: Use more direct acknowledgments combined with clarifying questions. "I heard you say work is frustrating. Help me understand specifically which parts feel most challenging right now."

Assumption 3: Ambivalence is normal and workable

Traditional MI expects ambivalence about change and treats it as a natural part of the process to explore and resolve.

Neurodivergent reality: Autistic individuals often experience less ambivalence and more clarity about what they want, but they may struggle with the social expectations or sensory demands of change rather than mixed feelings about the change itself. Their resistance might be practical rather than emotional.

ADHD individuals might feel certain about wanting change in the moment but struggle with the sustained attention and executive function demands required to implement changes over time. Their "ambivalence" might actually be realistic assessment of their brain's capabilities.

Better approach: Distinguish between emotional ambivalence and practical barriers. Ask directly about obstacles rather than assuming mixed feelings.

Assumption 4: People can identify and articulate their intrinsic motivations

MI assumes people can recognize and express what matters most to them when given the right conversational space.

Neurodivergent reality: Alexithymia—difficulty identifying and describing emotions—occurs in up to 50% of autistic individuals (Kinnaird et al., 2019). Asking someone who struggles with emotional awareness to identify their deepest motivations can be frustrating and unproductive.

ADHD individuals might have very clear motivations in the moment but struggle to access those same motivations when they're in a different emotional or energy state.

Better approach: Use concrete examples and behavioral observations to help people identify patterns in their motivations over time.

The neurodiversity-affirming approach to change conversations

A neurodiversity-affirming approach starts with a fundamental shift in perspective: neurodivergent traits aren't pathological symptoms to eliminate but natural variations that bring both strengths and challenges. This changes everything about how we approach change conversations.

Instead of: "How can we help you overcome your ADHD symptoms that interfere with your goals?"

Try: "How can we work with your ADHD brain to create systems that support your goals?"

This isn't just semantic politeness. The language reflects a deeper philosophical shift from a deficit model to a difference model. When we pathologize neurodivergent traits, we often end up fighting against the person's natural neurology. When we work with neurological differences, we can harness their strengths while providing support for genuine challenges.

Take stimming—repetitive movements that many autistic people engage in. Traditional approaches might view stimming as a behavior to reduce or eliminate. A neurodiversity-affirming approach recognizes stimming as a valuable self-regulation strategy and asks how to accommodate it rather than suppress it.

Marcus, a 28-year-old software developer with autism, rocks gently in his chair during therapy sessions. Instead of asking him to sit still, his therapist provides a rocking chair and notices that Marcus is most articulate and engaged when he can move rhythmically. The stimming isn't interfering with the conversation— it's supporting it.

Neurodiversity-affirming practice means adapting goals and settings to the person's natural communication and sensory patterns—rather than forcing "typical" behaviours like sustained eye contact or a single style of social reciprocity. Communication difficulties are often **bi-directional** between autistic and non-autistic people (the "double empathy problem"), and autistic-to-autistic communication can be highly effective; current consensus guidance describes what affirming practice should involve in therapy. (Milton, 2012; Crompton, Ropar, Evans-Williams, Flynn, & Fletcher-Watson, 2020; Flower et al., 2025). For ADHD individuals, this might mean acknowledging that their brains need more stimulation and variety to maintain engagement. Instead of viewing hyperactivity as problematic, we can frame it as energy that needs appropriate outlets.

Jennifer's ADHD makes traditional talk therapy feel painfully slow and unstimulating. Her counselor adapts by incorporating movement breaks, using visual tools, and allowing Jennifer to fidget with textured objects during sessions. Jennifer's therapy engagement improves dramatically when her sensory and movement needs are met.

The neurodiversity-affirming approach also recognizes that many challenges neurodivergent people face stem from environments and systems designed for neurotypical brains rather than from inherent deficits. This shifts the focus from "fixing" the person to improving the fit between the person and their environment.

Core principles of neurodivergent-adapted MI

Building on the foundation of neurodiversity-affirming practice, several core principles should guide motivational interviewing with neurodivergent individuals.

Principle 1: Assume competence and honor expertise

Neurodivergent individuals are experts on their own experience. This sounds obvious, but it's easy to slip into assuming that communication differences or processing variations indicate reduced insight or capability.

When someone takes longer to process information or expresses themselves differently, resist the urge to fill silence or interpret for them. Their different communication style doesn't indicate reduced intelligence or self-awareness.

In practice: Give people time to process questions. Some autistic individuals need several seconds to shift their attention to your question, process the language, formulate a response, and organize their thoughts into words. What feels like a long pause to you might be active, engaged thinking for them.

Ask directly about their expertise: "You've been living with ADHD for 25 years. What have you learned about what works and what doesn't work for your brain?"

Principle 2: Make the implicit explicit

Neurotypical communication relies heavily on implied meanings, social subtext, and unstated assumptions. Neurodivergent individuals often benefit when these implicit elements are made explicit.

Instead of hinting at what you're thinking, say it directly. Instead of assuming shared understanding, check it out. Instead of relying on nonverbal cues, use clear verbal communication.

In practice: "I'm going to ask you a question about your goals, and I'm hoping to understand what matters most to you. There's no right or wrong answer, and you can take as much time as you need to think about it."

This explicit framing helps neurodivergent individuals understand not just what you're asking but why you're asking and what kind of response you're looking for.

Principle 3: Provide structure within flexibility

Many neurodivergent individuals benefit from clear structure while still maintaining the collaborative spirit of MI. This isn't about becoming rigid or directive—it's about providing a framework that reduces cognitive load and anxiety.

Explain the structure of your conversation: "Today I'd like to understand more about what's working well in your life and what you'd like to be different. We'll probably spend about 20 minutes on each area. How does that sound to you?"

In practice: Use visual agendas, time estimates, and clear transitions between topics. Signal when you're shifting focus: "We've been talking about work for a while. I'd like to shift to discussing your home routines. Is that okay with you?"

Principle 4: Accommodate sensory and processing differences

Sensory processing differences can significantly impact a person's ability to engage in conversation. What seems like resistance or distraction might actually be sensory overwhelm or understimulation.

Pay attention to environmental factors: lighting, noise, temperature, seating, and space. Notice if someone seems uncomfortable and ask directly about their needs.

In practice: "I notice you keep looking toward the window. Would it help to move your chair or adjust the lighting?" or "Some people find it easier to talk while doing something with their hands. Would you like something to fidget with?"

Principle 5: Honor processing time and communication styles

Different brains process information at different speeds and in different ways. What looks like avoidance or resistance might be the brain taking the time it needs to do good work.

Some people think out loud and need to talk through their ideas to understand them. Others need quiet time to process internally before sharing their thoughts. Some communicate better in writing than verbally.

In practice: Offer multiple ways to engage: "Some people like to talk through their thoughts, and others prefer to think quietly first. What works better for your brain?" or "Would it help to write down some thoughts between now and next time we meet?"

Principle 6: Focus on functional goals over normative goals

The goal isn't to make neurodivergent people more neurotypical—it's to help them function well and feel satisfied with their lives as neurodivergent people.

This means paying attention to whether goals are driven by the person's genuine values or by pressure to conform to neurotypical expectations.

In practice: When someone says they want to "be more social," explore what that means to them specifically. Do they want more social connection, or do they feel pressured to socialize in neurotypical ways? Maybe they'd be happier with one deep friendship than a large social circle, or they'd prefer online communities over face-to-face socializing.

Principle 7: Work with, not against, neurodivergent traits

Many neurodivergent traits that are often pathologized can actually be leveraged as strengths when properly supported.

Autistic attention to detail and pattern recognition can be powerful tools for tracking progress and identifying what works. ADHD hyperfocus can drive intense bursts of productive change when properly channeled. Executive function challenges can be addressed with external systems and supports rather than trying to develop neurotypical executive skills.

In practice: "I notice you're incredibly detailed in how you track your moods. That's a real strength. How could we use that same attention to detail to track your progress toward your goals?"

These principles create a foundation for motivational interviewing that honors neurodivergent brains rather than trying to force them into neurotypical patterns. The goal isn't to abandon the spirit of MI but to adapt its techniques to work with different neurological realities.

When we make these adaptations, something remarkable happens: not only do neurodivergent individuals engage more fully in change conversations, but many of these adaptations actually benefit neurotypical people too. Clearer communication, explicit structure, and sensory awareness improve conversations for everyone.

The next chapter will explore how sensory processing differences impact communication and how to create environments that support rather than hinder meaningful change conversations. Because before we can engage someone's mind, we need to ensure their sensory system isn't overwhelmed or understimulated to the point where higher-level thinking becomes impossible.

What we've covered so far

Understanding neurodivergent brains requires us to fundamentally reconsider our assumptions about communication, motivation, and change. Traditional MI techniques that work well for neurotypical individuals can create unnecessary barriers when applied without modification to autistic and ADHD brains.

The key insight is that neurodivergent brains aren't defective—they're different. When we adapt our approach to work with these differences rather than against them, we can engage in more effective and respectful change conversations.

This means making implicit communication explicit, providing structure within flexibility, accommodating processing differences, and focusing on functional rather than normative goals. Most importantly, it means assuming competence and honoring the expertise that comes from living with a neurodivergent brain.

Chapter 2: Sensory-Aware MI

Environmental adaptations for success

Dr. Martinez scheduled her first session with Alex, a 16-year-old with autism, in her usual office. Fluorescent lights hummed overhead, traffic noise filtered through thin windows, and the air conditioning cycled on and off with a mechanical whir. Alex walked in, immediately squinted at the lights, and within five minutes was rocking back and forth with his hands pressed firmly against his ears.

"I can't think in here," he said, his voice strained. "Everything is too much."

Dr. Martinez had spent years learning motivational interviewing techniques, but she'd never considered how the sensory environment might determine whether those techniques could work at all. Alex's brain was spending so much energy managing sensory input that it had little capacity left for the higher-level thinking required in therapy conversations.

The session that was supposed to explore Alex's goals and motivations instead became an exercise in sensory survival.

This scenario plays out daily in offices, schools, and homes where well-intentioned helpers try to engage neurodivergent individuals in change conversations without considering the sensory foundation that makes such conversations possible.

Sensory processing differences and their impact on communication

Before diving into environmental modifications, we need to understand what's happening in neurodivergent brains when they encounter sensory input. For many neurodivergent individuals, what seems like a normal environment to neurotypical people can feel like trying to have a conversation while standing next to a construction site or in a funhouse full of distracting mirrors.

Sensory processing differences affect approximately 90% of autistic individuals and up to 40% of people with ADHD (Ben-Sasson et al., 2009). These differences can manifest as hypersensitivity (over-responsiveness), hyposensitivity (under-responsiveness), or seeking behaviors where people actively pursue intense sensory input.

Hypersensitivity: When the world feels too much

Maya, a 22-year-old college student with autism, describes fluorescent lights as "angry bees buzzing inside my skull." The barely noticeable flicker that most people tune out becomes a constant, intrusive presence that makes concentration nearly impossible. During therapy sessions under fluorescent lighting, Maya struggles to access her thoughts and articulate her feelings—not because she lacks insight, but because her brain is working overtime to manage the sensory assault.

Hypersensitivity can affect any sensory channel:

Auditory: Background noise that neurotypical people filter out—air conditioning, traffic, conversation from other rooms—can feel overwhelming and intrusive. Some autistic individuals report that they can't filter competing sounds, so they hear everything with equal intensity.

Visual: Bright lights, flickering screens, busy patterns, or too much visual information can cause genuine physical discomfort and cognitive overload.

Tactile: Certain textures, temperatures, or clothing can feel intensely uncomfortable. Even the feeling of air movement from heating systems can be distracting.

Olfactory: Strong scents, cleaning products, or even subtle smells that others don't notice can be nauseating or overwhelming.

Proprioceptive: Some people have difficulty sensing where their body is in space, making certain seating arrangements or room layouts feel disorienting.

When someone is experiencing sensory overload, their brain's higher-level executive functions—the very capacities needed for reflection, planning, and change conversations—become significantly compromised. It's not that they don't want to engage; it's that their nervous system is in survival mode.

Hyposensitivity: When the world feels too little

Jason, a 35-year-old with ADHD, feels most alert and focused in environments that would overwhelm other people. He works best with music playing, multiple browser tabs open, and his phone nearby. In quiet, understimulated environments, his brain starts seeking stimulation wherever it can find it—leading to what looks like distraction but is actually his brain trying to reach an optimal arousal level.

Hyposensitivity can also affect multiple sensory channels:

Vestibular: Need for movement and position changes to maintain alertness and focus

Proprioceptive: Requiring stronger physical input—tight hugs, weighted blankets, or pressure—to feel grounded

Auditory: Needing background noise or music to concentrate rather than finding it distracting

Visual: Requiring bright lights or high contrast to maintain visual attention

Understanding these differences is crucial because traditional therapy environments are typically designed to minimize sensory input—quiet rooms, neutral colors, soft lighting. While this works well for neurotypical clients who might find stimulation distracting, it can actually impair the functioning of neurodivergent individuals who need different sensory conditions to think clearly.

16

Creating sensory-friendly conversation environments

The goal isn't to create a perfectly neutral environment (which is impossible anyway) but to create an environment that works for the specific individual you're working with. This requires direct conversation about sensory needs and often some experimentation.

The sensory assessment conversation

Start every new relationship with explicit conversation about environmental needs. Most neurodivergent individuals have strong awareness of what helps and what hurts, but they're not always asked about it.

"Before we start talking about your goals, I want to make sure this space works for your brain. Some people focus better with background noise, others need it quiet. Some people like bright lights, others prefer it dimmer. What works best for you?"

This conversation serves multiple purposes: it communicates that you understand sensory processing differences matter, it positions the person as the expert on their own needs, and it demonstrates that you're willing to adapt your approach.

Ask specifically about different sensory channels:

- **Lighting:** "How do these lights feel? Would you prefer them brighter, dimmer, or different somehow?"

- **Sound:** "How is the noise level? Do you focus better with some background sound or complete quiet?"

- **Seating:** "How does that chair work for you? Some people prefer to stand or move around during conversations."

- **Temperature:** "Is the temperature comfortable? Some people think better when it's cooler or warmer."

- **Scents:** "Do you notice any smells that are distracting or uncomfortable?"

Flexible environmental options

Create multiple options within your space rather than one "perfect" setup. Different people need different conditions, and the same person might need different conditions on different days depending on their stress level, sleep, and other factors.

Lighting options:

- Natural light from windows when possible

- Adjustable lamps instead of or in addition to overhead lighting

- Option to turn off fluorescent lights

- Colored bulbs or filters for people who find certain light frequencies painful

Seating variety:

- Traditional chairs and a couch

- Standing desk or high table option

- Balance ball or rocking chair for people who need movement

- Floor cushions or beanbag chairs for those who prefer different positions

- Weighted lap pads for proprioceptive input

Sound management:

- White noise machine or fan for consistent background sound

- Noise-canceling headphones available

- Soft instrumental music option

- Complete quiet when needed

Fidget and sensory tools:

- Stress balls, fidget cubes, or thinking putty

- Textured fabric or sensory strips attached to table edges
- Weighted items for lap pressure
- Chewable jewelry or tools for people who need oral input

Timing and pacing considerations

Sensory processing capacity fluctuates throughout the day and can be affected by stress, fatigue, and other factors. What works in a morning session might not work in an afternoon session.

Pay attention to signs of sensory overload or understimulation:

Overload signs:

- Increased rocking, fidgeting, or self-soothing behaviors
- Covering ears or closing eyes
- Withdrawing from conversation or becoming monosyllabic
- Increased irritability or emotional reactivity
- Physical signs of stress (tense posture, rapid breathing)

Understimulation signs:

- Difficulty maintaining attention or focus
- Seeking additional sensory input (tapping, movement, sound)
- Appearing "checked out" or distracted
- Restlessness or inability to sit still

When you notice these signs, address them directly rather than pushing through: "I notice you seem uncomfortable. What would help right now? Should we adjust something in the environment or take a break?"

Adapting MI techniques for sensory sensitivities

Traditional MI techniques often need modification to accommodate sensory processing differences. The core spirit of MI remains the same, but the delivery methods change.

Modified eye contact expectations

Traditional MI emphasizes eye contact as a way to build connection and demonstrate attention. For many autistic individuals, sustained eye contact is uncomfortable, distracting, or even painful.

Instead of insisting on eye contact, focus on other indicators of engagement:

- Body orientation toward you
- Responsive verbal communication
- Asking questions or making comments
- Fidgeting that indicates processing rather than disengagement

Let the person know that eye contact isn't required: "Some people focus better when they're looking at their hands or looking around the room rather than maintaining eye contact. Whatever helps you think clearly is fine with me."

Accommodating movement needs

Many neurodivergent individuals think better when they can move. Instead of viewing fidgeting or movement as distraction, recognize it as a self-regulation strategy that often enhances rather than impairs thinking.

Encourage beneficial movement:

"Feel free to get up and walk around if that helps you think."

"Some people focus better when their hands are busy. Would you like something to fidget with?"

Incorporate movement into techniques:

Instead of: "Let's talk about your goals while sitting here."

Try: "Some people think better while walking. Would you like to have this conversation while we walk around the building?"

Adjusting reflective listening

Standard reflective listening often involves paraphrasing what someone has said using slightly different words. For autistic individuals who process language very precisely, this can feel like you're misunderstanding or changing their meaning.

Adapt your reflective listening style:

Use their exact words when possible: "You said work feels 'overwhelming,' not just difficult. Tell me more about overwhelming specifically."

Ask permission before paraphrasing: "Let me see if I understand what you're saying. You feel like... Does that capture it, or would you say it differently?"

Check for understanding rather than assuming: "I want to make sure I understand correctly. When you say X, do you mean Y, or something else?"

Sensory-aware scaling questions

Traditional scaling questions ask people to rate things on a numerical scale: "On a scale of 1 to 10, how important is this goal to you?" While these can work well for neurodivergent individuals, consider adding sensory or concrete anchors to make the scales more meaningful.

Visual scales: Create physical scales with colors, shapes, or images rather than just numbers.

Embodied scales: "Show me with your hands how big this problem feels" or "If this goal was a sound, would it be a whisper or a shout?"

Concrete comparisons: "Is this goal more important than getting good sleep, less important, or about the same?"

When to modify, pause, or reschedule conversations

Recognizing when sensory processing differences are interfering with meaningful conversation is crucial. Sometimes the most respectful and effective intervention is to stop and address environmental needs rather than pushing forward with content.

Signs that environmental modification is needed

Immediate indicators:

- Person repeatedly asks "what?" or seems unable to process questions they would normally understand

- Visible signs of sensory distress (covering ears, squinting, physical tension)

- Sudden changes in communication style or emotional regulation

- Statements like "I can't think" or "everything feels loud/bright/too much"

Gradual indicators:

- Decreasing engagement over the course of the session

- Increasing fidgeting, rocking, or self-soothing behaviors

- Responses becoming shorter or less detailed

- Person seeming "checked out" or distracted despite previous engagement

The environmental check-in

When you notice these signs, address them directly:

"I notice you seem uncomfortable. How is the environment feeling right now?"

"Something seems different about your energy. Do we need to adjust anything in the room?"

"Your brain seems like it might be working hard to manage something. What would help right now?"

When to pause or reschedule

Sometimes environmental modifications aren't enough, and the most respectful choice is to pause or reschedule the conversation.

Consider pausing when:

- Environmental modifications don't resolve the sensory distress

- The person reports feeling overwhelmed or unable to think clearly

- You're not able to create appropriate environmental conditions in the moment

Frame pausing positively:

"It sounds like your brain is working really hard right now to manage sensory input. That doesn't leave much capacity for the kind of thinking we want to do together. Would it work better to meet again when we can set up the environment differently?"

This isn't giving up—it's recognizing that meaningful change conversations require optimal conditions for each individual's brain.

Creating sensory-friendly scheduling

Consider scheduling factors that might affect sensory processing:

Time of day: Some people have better sensory tolerance in mornings, others in afternoons. Ask about preferences.

Day of week: Monday morning might feel very different from Friday afternoon in terms of sensory capacity.

Season and weather: Barometric pressure changes, seasonal light differences, and weather can all impact sensory processing.

Life circumstances: High stress periods, changes in routine, or other life events can reduce sensory processing capacity.

The goal is creating conditions where neurodivergent individuals can bring their best thinking and authentic engagement to change conversations. When we pay attention to sensory processing needs, we often find that people who seemed resistant or unmotivated are actually highly capable and insightful—they just needed environmental conditions that worked with rather than against their neurology.

In the next chapter, we'll explore how differences in information processing speed and working memory require us to adapt the pacing and structure of motivational interviewing conversations. Because even in optimal sensory environments, neurodivergent brains often need different timing and organizational approaches to engage fully with change-focused discussions.

Taking it further

Environmental awareness transforms therapeutic relationships with neurodivergent individuals. When we create sensory-friendly spaces and adapt our techniques accordingly, we remove barriers that have nothing to do with motivation or capacity and everything to do with neurological differences.

The key is recognizing that sensory processing differences aren't secondary concerns to address if you have time—they're foundational requirements for meaningful engagement. A person can't access their motivation, explore their ambivalence, or commit to change when their nervous system is in survival mode due to sensory overload or understimulation.

This chapter's principles benefit everyone, not just neurodivergent individuals. Creating flexible, responsive environments and paying attention to sensory needs improves communication and engagement across neurological differences.

Chapter 3: Processing Differences

Pacing and structure modifications

Rebecca, a skilled therapist trained in motivational interviewing, felt frustrated after her third session with David, a brilliant 32-year-old engineer with ADHD. She'd ask a thoughtful open-ended question about his goals, then watch as David's eyes would glaze over mid-conversation. He'd start responding enthusiastically, then trail off and seem to forget what they were discussing. When she tried to reflect back what she'd heard, David would interrupt with "Yeah, yeah, I know that already" and jump to an entirely different topic.

Rebecca wondered if David was unmotivated or resistant to change. What she didn't realize was that David's brain was processing information at a completely different speed and in a fundamentally different pattern than traditional MI techniques assume. His apparent distraction and topic-jumping weren't signs of disengagement—they were signs of a brain that processes information rapidly but struggles with the sustained attention and working memory demands of linear, slow-paced therapeutic conversation.

The solution wasn't to change David's motivation. It was to adapt the conversation's pacing and structure to match how his brain actually works.

Information processing speed variations

Neurodivergent brains often process information at dramatically different speeds than neurotypical brains—sometimes much faster, sometimes much slower, and often inconsistently depending on the topic, interest level, and current cognitive load.

ADHD and rapid processing

Many people with ADHD think at lightning speed. Their brains make rapid connections between ideas, jump quickly from concept to concept, and can become impatient with the slower pace of traditional therapeutic conversation.

Kevin, a 28-year-old with ADHD, describes his thinking process: "It's like my brain is a race car being asked to drive through a school zone. I can see the destination clearly, I know exactly where I want to go, but I have to creep along at this painfully slow pace that makes me want to jump out of my skin."

When we try to conduct traditional MI with rapid processors, several problems emerge:

Impatience with reflection: By the time you're reflecting back what they said two minutes ago, they've already thought through that concept thoroughly and moved on to three related ideas.

Topic jumping: Their brain makes connections faster than they can verbally explain, leading to conversation that seems scattered but actually follows a logical (if rapid) internal process.

Interrupting: Not because they're rude, but because they've already processed your complete thought and are ready to respond before you finish speaking.

Apparent inattention: They might seem to stop listening, but actually they heard your point immediately and their brain has moved on to processing implications and responses.

Autism and processing depth

Many autistic individuals process information more slowly but with greater depth and precision. They might need extended time to fully understand a question, access relevant information from their memory, and formulate a thoughtful response.

Sarah, a 25-year-old autistic graduate student, explains: "When someone asks me a question, I don't just think about the surface answer. I think about all the possible interpretations of the question, what context might be relevant, what exceptions there might be, and how my answer connects to everything else we've discussed. That takes time, but it also means my answer is usually more accurate and complete."

Processing differences in autism often include:

Longer response time: What feels like a long pause to you might be active, engaged thinking for them.

Need for precision: They may ask clarifying questions or seem to over-think simple questions because they want to provide accurate, complete responses.

Difficulty with interruption: If you interrupt their thinking process to move the conversation along, they may lose their train of thought entirely and need to start over.

Context switching challenges: Moving between topics requires mental energy and time to shift cognitive gears.

Variable processing based on interest and energy

For both ADHD and autistic individuals, processing speed can vary dramatically based on topic interest, current energy level, and cognitive load.

Interest-based processing: Topics that align with personal interests or expertise are processed much more quickly and thoroughly than topics that feel boring or irrelevant.

Energy-dependent processing: When tired, stressed, or overwhelmed, processing speed can slow significantly for everyone, but particularly for neurodivergent individuals.

Executive function load: If someone is already managing multiple cognitive tasks (remembering appointments, processing sensory input, managing social interaction), they have less processing capacity available for therapeutic conversation.

Working memory considerations in MI conversations

Working memory—the ability to hold and manipulate information in your mind while using it—functions differently in neurodivergent brains. Traditional MI techniques often assume robust working memory capacity that many neurodivergent individuals don't have.

ADHD working memory challenges

People with ADHD typically have significantly reduced working memory capacity (Kasper et al., 2012). This affects therapeutic conversation in several ways:

Forgetting the original question: By the time they've thought through their response, they may have forgotten what you originally asked.

Losing track of conversation threads: In a 45-minute session covering multiple topics, they might lose track of how different pieces connect together.

Difficulty with complex reflections: If you reflect back several different points they made, they might only be able to process one or two elements at a time.

Overwhelm with too much information: Providing too many options or too much information at once can cause their working memory to become overloaded.

Marcus demonstrates this during a session about work-life balance: His therapist asks about his goals for managing stress. Marcus starts explaining about his work deadlines, then mentions his exercise routine, then talks about his relationship, then circles back to work but seems confused about how these topics connect. By the end of his explanation, neither he nor his therapist can remember the original question about stress management goals.

Autism working memory patterns

Autistic individuals often have different working memory patterns rather than simply reduced capacity. They might have excellent working memory for detailed information in their areas of interest but struggle with working memory for social or emotional information.

Detail-rich processing: They might remember extraordinarily specific details about previous conversations but struggle to hold multiple abstract concepts in mind simultaneously.

Sequential processing: They may need to work through information in a specific order and become confused if topics are presented in a different sequence than their brain processes them.

Context-dependent memory: Information might be stored with very specific contextual details, making it harder to access in different contexts.

Adapting for working memory differences

External working memory supports become essential for successful MI with neurodivergent individuals. Instead of expecting people to hold complex information in their minds, provide external systems to support their thinking.

Written agendas and notes:

- Provide a written agenda at the beginning of each session
- Take notes during the conversation that both of you can see
- Write down key goals, insights, or commitments rather than expecting people to remember them

Visual organizers:

- Use charts, diagrams, or mind maps to show how different topics connect

- Create visual scales for rating importance, confidence, or progress
- Use color coding to organize different types of information

Chunk information:

- Break complex topics into smaller, manageable pieces
- Address one concept thoroughly before moving to the next
- Provide clear transitions between topics

Frequent summarizing:

- Summarize key points regularly rather than waiting until the end
- Ask the person to summarize in their own words to check understanding
- Create written summaries that can be referenced later

Providing structure while maintaining MI spirit

One of the biggest challenges in neurodivergent-adapted MI is providing the additional structure that supports different processing styles while maintaining the collaborative, non-directive spirit of motivational interviewing. The goal isn't to become directive or prescriptive but to create scaffolding that supports the person's own exploration and decision-making.

Structured flexibility approach

Think of structure as providing a helpful framework rather than rigid requirements. Like a trellis that supports a climbing plant—it provides guidance and support while allowing natural growth in the person's own direction.

Session structure that maintains MI spirit:

1. **Opening structure:** "Today I'd like to understand more about [topic you agreed on previously]. We'll probably spend about 20 minutes exploring what's working well and 20 minutes discussing what you'd like to change. How does that sound to you?"

2. **Topic organization:** "I hear you mentioning three different areas—work, family, and health. Which one feels most important to focus on first?"

3. **Transition warnings:** "We've been talking about work challenges for a while, and I'm curious about the family situation you mentioned. Is it okay if we shift to that, or do you want to finish this thought first?"

4. **Progress checking:** "We're about halfway through our time today. How is this conversation feeling for you so far?"

Explicit process explanations

Many neurodivergent individuals engage more fully when they understand not just what you're doing but why you're doing it. Make your MI process transparent.

Instead of: "Tell me about a time when things were going well."

Try: "I'm going to ask you about a time when things were going well because sometimes understanding what worked in the past can help us think about what might work in the future. Tell me about a time when things were going well."

Instead of: "What would need to change for you to feel more motivated?"

Try: "I want to understand what factors affect your motivation because you're the expert on what works for your brain. What would need to change for you to feel more motivated?"

This transparency serves multiple purposes:

- Reduces anxiety about hidden agendas or unclear expectations

- Helps people understand their role in the conversation
- Allows people to engage more intentionally with the process
- Respects their intelligence and autonomy

Choice within structure

Provide structure that includes multiple options rather than single paths. This maintains the collaborative nature of MI while providing the organization that supports different processing styles.

Structured choice examples:

"I'd like to understand your goals better. Some people like to think about what they want their life to look like in the future, others prefer to think about problems they want to solve, and others like to start with what's already working well. Which approach sounds most interesting to your brain?"

"We could explore this by talking through your thoughts, drawing a picture or diagram, or doing a pros and cons list. What sounds most helpful?"

"Some people process by thinking out loud, others need quiet time to think, and others like to move around while they think. What helps your brain work best?"

Predictable unpredictability

Create consistent structures that can accommodate inconsistent processing patterns. Neurodivergent individuals often benefit from knowing what to expect while having flexibility for how their brain shows up on any given day.

Consistent session opening:

- Check in about environmental needs
- Brief review of previous session or agenda
- Agreement about focus for current session

- Reminder about time frame and structure

Flexible middle:

- Adapt pacing to current processing speed

- Follow the person's energy and interest

- Use whatever processing modalities work best in the moment

Consistent closing:

- Summarize key insights or commitments

- Check about next steps or follow-up

- Brief preview of next session if scheduled

Time flexibility and conversation pacing strategies

Traditional therapy operates on fixed 45-50 minute sessions with predetermined pacing. Neurodivergent brains often need different timing structures to engage effectively with change conversations.

ADHD pacing needs

ADHD brains often need faster pacing and more variety to maintain engagement. Long, slow explorations of single topics can cause attention to drift and energy to drop.

Faster topic rotation: Instead of spending 45 minutes on one goal, spend 15 minutes each on three related goals, allowing for rapid topic changes that match natural ADHD thinking patterns.

Energy-based pacing: Pay attention to engagement and energy levels. When energy drops, either change topics, take a movement break, or introduce a more stimulating activity.

Interest-driven timing: Spend more time on topics that capture natural interest and less time on topics that feel boring, even if the boring topics seem more "important" from an outside perspective.

Activity breaks: Build in movement breaks or hands-on activities every 15-20 minutes to help maintain attention and engagement.

Jake, a 34-year-old with ADHD, works best with sessions structured like this:

- 10 minutes: Check-in and agenda setting

- 15 minutes: High-interest topic exploration

- 5 minutes: Movement break or fidget activity

- 15 minutes: Problem-solving or planning

- 5 minutes: Summary and next steps

Autism pacing needs

Autistic individuals often need slower pacing and more processing time. Rushing through topics or pressuring for quick responses can impair their ability to access their thoughts and communicate effectively.

Extended processing time: Allow longer pauses after questions. What feels like an uncomfortable silence to you might be productive thinking time for them.

Topic depth over breadth: Rather than covering many topics superficially, explore fewer topics with greater depth and thoroughness.

Transition time: Build in time for mental transitions between topics. Announce topic changes in advance and allow time for cognitive gear-shifting.

Reduced interruptions: Avoid interrupting their thinking or speaking process, even if their response seems complete to you.

Maria, a 29-year-old autistic woman, engages best with sessions like this:

- 5 minutes: Settling in and sensory adjustment

- 20 minutes: Deep exploration of one primary topic with minimal interruption

- 10 minutes: Processing break or related activity

- 15 minutes: Practical planning and next steps related to the primary topic

Flexible scheduling options

Consider alternatives to traditional weekly 45-minute sessions that might better match neurodivergent processing styles.

Intensive sessions: Some people work better with longer, less frequent sessions that allow for deeper exploration without the overhead of re-establishing context each week.

Brief frequent contacts: Others benefit from shorter, more frequent check-ins that provide regular support without overwhelming their processing capacity.

Variable timing: Allow session length to vary based on the person's processing needs and energy on a given day. Some sessions might be 30 minutes, others might be 60 minutes.

Asynchronous elements: Include between-session communication through email, texts, or shared documents that allow people to process and respond at their own pace.

Managing processing overload

Recognize signs that someone's processing capacity is becoming overwhelmed and adjust accordingly.

Overload indicators:

- Responses becoming shorter or less detailed

- Increased fidgeting or self-soothing behaviors

- Difficulty following conversation threads

- Asking to repeat questions they would normally understand
- Seeming "checked out" or distracted

Overload responses:
- Slow down the pace of conversation
- Reduce the amount of new information being introduced
- Take a processing break
- Simplify complex topics into smaller components
- Offer to pause and resume later

The goal is creating conversation conditions that allow neurodivergent brains to operate at their optimal capacity rather than forcing them to function under suboptimal processing conditions.

When we adapt our pacing and structure to match different processing styles, we often discover that people who seemed unmotivated or resistant are actually highly engaged and insightful—they just needed conversation conditions that matched their neurological reality.

The next section of this book will focus specifically on adaptations for autism spectrum differences, starting with how to modify traditional MI language and communication styles to work effectively with literal, concrete thinking patterns.

Moving forward effectively

Processing differences aren't obstacles to overcome—they're neurological realities to work with skillfully. When we adapt our pacing and structure to match how different brains actually process information, we create conditions for more effective and respectful change conversations.

The key insight is that the same conversation content can be delivered in multiple ways. By providing appropriate structure, managing working memory demands, and adjusting our timing to match individual processing patterns, we enable neurodivergent individuals to bring their full capacity to change-focused discussions.

These adaptations often benefit neurotypical individuals as well. Clear structure, explicit process explanations, and flexible pacing improve therapeutic engagement across neurological differences.

Chapter 4: Literal Language MI

Concrete communication strategies

Dr. Chen had been practicing motivational interviewing for fifteen years when she met Emma, a 24-year-old autistic woman seeking help with career decisions. Following her standard MI training, Dr. Chen opened with a warm, exploratory question: "So Emma, what brings you here today?"

Emma shifted uncomfortably in her chair and asked, "Do you mean what mode of transportation I used to get here? I took the bus. Or are you asking about my motivation for scheduling this appointment? Or perhaps you want to know about the sequence of events that led to me being in this specific location at this time?"

Dr. Chen realized she'd made an assumption that would color the entire therapeutic relationship. Emma wasn't being difficult or overly literal to be challenging—she was processing language exactly as her brain naturally works. The open-ended, metaphorical language that neurotypical clients find inviting and expansive felt confusing and overwhelming to Emma's more concrete, precise thinking style.

This interaction changed everything about how Dr. Chen approached language in therapy. She discovered that clear, direct communication wasn't less empathetic—it was more respectful of how Emma's brain actually processes information.

Moving from abstract to concrete language

Traditional motivational interviewing relies heavily on abstract concepts and open-ended exploration. Phrases like "Tell me about your relationship with change" or "What does success mean to you?" assume that people naturally think in abstract, conceptual terms. For many autistic individuals, this assumption creates unnecessary barriers to meaningful conversation.

Abstract thinking isn't absent in autism—it's often processed differently. Many autistic people are capable of sophisticated abstract reasoning, but they frequently prefer to work from concrete details toward abstract concepts rather than starting with abstract ideas and working backward.

The concrete-to-abstract bridge

Instead of beginning with abstract questions, start with specific, concrete details and build toward broader concepts. This approach respects how many autistic brains naturally process information while still reaching the same therapeutic goals.

Traditional abstract approach: "Tell me about your goals for therapy."

Concrete bridge approach: "What specific things in your daily life would you like to be different? For example, what happens on a typical Tuesday that you wish happened differently?"

Starting with concrete Tuesday details allows the person to access specific, observable experiences. From there, you can help them identify patterns and abstract principles, but you're working with their natural processing flow rather than against it.

Jason, a 28-year-old autistic engineer, struggled when his therapist asked about his "relationship with stress." The phrase "relationship with stress" felt meaningless to him. But when asked, "What does your body feel like when you're stressed? What thoughts go through your mind? What do you do differently?" he could provide detailed, specific answers. From these concrete details, together they identified patterns and developed a clearer understanding of how stress affected his life.

Operational definitions for therapeutic concepts

Many MI concepts that seem straightforward to neurotypical people require explicit definition and concrete examples for

autistic individuals. Instead of assuming shared understanding, provide clear operational definitions.

Motivation: Instead of asking "How motivated are you?" ask "On a scale of 1 to 10, how likely are you to actually do this specific action in the next week?"

Confidence: Instead of "How confident do you feel?" ask "If you had to do this task right now, how many steps of the process could you complete successfully?"

Readiness: Instead of "Are you ready to change?" ask "What specific actions are you willing to take between now and next week?"

Values: Instead of "What are your core values?" ask "When you feel most satisfied with your life, what specific things are happening? What are you doing? Who are you with? What does your day look like?"

Specificity in questioning techniques

Replace vague, open-ended questions with specific, concrete inquiries that still honor the person's autonomy and expertise.

Vague: "How do you feel about this situation?" **Specific:** "When you think about this situation, what physical sensations do you notice in your body? What thoughts come to mind? What emotions can you identify?"

Vague: "What would you like to work on?" **Specific:** "What specific behavior would you like to do more often, less often, or differently? What specific situation would you like to handle better?"

Vague: "Tell me about your support system." **Specific:** "Who are the people you talk to when you're having a difficult day? Who helps you with practical tasks? Who do you spend time with for enjoyment?"

This approach provides the same rich information as traditional open-ended questions but in a format that's more accessible to concrete thinking styles.

Avoiding metaphors and unclear expressions

Metaphorical language that enhances communication for neurotypical individuals can create confusion and misunderstanding for autistic people. Common therapeutic metaphors often require interpretation skills that don't align with literal thinking patterns.

Common problematic metaphors in MI

"Opening doors" to new possibilities: For someone who thinks literally, this might create confusion about actual doors, or they might wonder why doors need to be opened to discuss abstract concepts.

"Building bridges" between different parts of life: This architectural metaphor might prompt questions about construction materials, engineering specifications, or geographical locations rather than fostering thinking about connections between life domains.

"Breaking down barriers" to change: The violent imagery of "breaking" and "barriers" might feel aggressive or confusing rather than inspiring.

"Planting seeds" for future growth: Agricultural metaphors assume familiarity with gardening processes and seasonal timelines that may not translate meaningfully.

Clear alternatives to common metaphors

Instead of: "What barriers are preventing you from reaching your goals?" **Try:** "What specific obstacles make it difficult to achieve your goals? What gets in the way?"

Instead of: "Let's explore what resonates with you." **Try:** "Which of these options feels most interesting or appealing to you?"

Instead of: "How can we bridge the gap between where you are and where you want to be?" **Try:** "What specific steps would move you from your current situation toward your goal?"

Instead of: "What's your gut feeling about this?" **Try:** "What's your immediate reaction? What do you think about this option?"

When metaphors can work

Some autistic individuals enjoy and connect with metaphors, particularly when the metaphors relate to their special interests or areas of expertise. The key is checking whether metaphorical language is helpful rather than assuming it will be.

Test metaphor effectiveness directly: "I sometimes use the metaphor of a toolbox when talking about coping strategies— different tools for different problems. Does that way of thinking about it make sense to you, or would you prefer a different way to organize these ideas?"

Use person-specific metaphors: If someone is passionate about computer programming, software metaphors might be helpful. If they're interested in music, musical metaphors might resonate. But base this on their interests, not general assumptions.

Direct communication while maintaining empathy

One of the biggest concerns people have about adapting MI for autism is whether direct, concrete communication can maintain the warmth and empathy that are central to effective therapeutic relationships. The concern is understandable but misguided—direct communication is often more empathetic for autistic individuals because it reduces confusion, anxiety, and cognitive load.

Warmth through clarity

For many autistic people, clear communication demonstrates respect and care more effectively than warm but ambiguous language. When you speak clearly and directly, you're honoring their communication style and reducing the social interpretation work they have to do.

Traditional empathetic response: "It sounds like you're really struggling with some difficult feelings about this situation."

Clear empathetic response: "You said you feel frustrated and anxious about your job situation. Those feelings make sense given what you're dealing with."

The second response validates the specific emotions the person named, demonstrates that you heard them accurately, and affirms that their response is understandable. This approach often feels more supportive to autistic individuals because it's based on their actual words rather than your interpretation of their words.

Emotional validation through specificity

Validate emotions by referencing specific details rather than making general statements about feelings.

Generic validation: "That must be really hard for you."

Specific validation: "You mentioned feeling exhausted after social interactions at work and then not having energy for activities you enjoy at home. That schedule sounds genuinely difficult to manage."

Specific validation demonstrates that you're paying attention to their actual experience rather than responding with generic therapeutic phrases.

Expressing empathy without ambiguity

Empathetic responses can be both warm and clear when they're based on the person's specific experience.

"Based on what you've told me, it makes perfect sense that you'd feel overwhelmed. Managing a full-time job, taking care of your family, and dealing with unexpected changes in your routine would be challenging for anyone."

This response is empathetic because it:

- Acknowledges their specific circumstances

- Normalizes their emotional response

- Demonstrates understanding of the cumulative impact of multiple stressors

Asking permission for emotional processing

Rather than assuming what someone needs emotionally, ask directly about their preferences for processing feelings.

"You've shared some information about a difficult situation at work. Some people like to talk through their feelings about situations like this, others prefer to focus on problem-solving, and some people need time to process internally before discussing emotions. What feels most helpful to you right now?"

This approach respects their autonomy while offering multiple ways to engage with emotional content.

Clarifying ambiguous MI concepts

Many core MI concepts require explicit clarification when working with autistic individuals. Rather than assuming shared understanding of therapeutic terminology, provide clear definitions and examples.

Ambivalence clarification

Traditional MI: "It sounds like you have mixed feelings about this decision."

Clarified approach: "It sounds like part of you wants to make this change because [specific benefits they mentioned], and part of you has concerns because [specific concerns they mentioned]. Is that accurate?"

Follow up with: "When you think about the part of you that wants to make this change, what specific benefits do you imagine? When you think about the part that has concerns, what specific problems do you worry about?"

Change talk identification

Rather than using the abstract concept of "change talk," help people recognize and understand their own motivation patterns.

"I notice that when you talk about [specific goal], your voice has more energy and you provide more details. When you talk about [different topic], you seem less engaged. What do you think accounts for that difference?"

This helps people understand their own motivation patterns without requiring them to understand the theoretical concept of change talk.

Values clarification exercises

Traditional values exercises often use abstract words that can feel meaningless to concrete thinkers. Create values exercises that use specific behavioral examples.

Instead of: "What values are most important to you?"

Try: "Think about a day in the past month when you felt satisfied with how you spent your time. What specifically were you doing? Who were you with? What about that day felt good to you?"

Then: "Think about a day when you felt unsatisfied or frustrated with how you spent your time. What was different about that day? What was missing or what happened that felt wrong?"

From these specific examples, you can help identify value patterns: "It sounds like days that include [specific activities/people/circumstances] tend to feel more satisfying to you. Does that match your experience?"

Goal-setting precision

Help people set goals that are specific, measurable, and behaviorally defined rather than abstract or aspirational.

Vague goal: "I want to be less anxious."

Concrete goal development:

1. "What specific situations make you feel most anxious?"

2. "In those situations, what would you like to be able to do differently?"

3. "What would success look like? How would you know you were handling anxiety better?"

4. "What specific changes in your thoughts, feelings, or behaviors would indicate improvement?"

This process transforms abstract goals into concrete, actionable objectives that align with literal thinking styles.

Progress measurement

Create clear, specific ways to measure progress rather than relying on subjective feelings or general impressions.

Instead of: "How are things going with your goal?"

Try: "Last week you wanted to [specific behavioral goal]. How many times did you do [specific behavior]? What situations made it easier or harder to follow through?"

Track specific behaviors: "You wanted to speak up in meetings at work. This week, how many meetings did you attend? In how many of those meetings did you contribute a comment or question?"

Use concrete comparisons: "Two weeks ago, you said social events felt overwhelming after about 30 minutes. How long were you able to stay engaged at this week's social events? What helped you stay longer, or what made you need to leave earlier?"

Resistance and ambivalence reframing

When someone seems resistant or ambivalent, explore the specific practical and emotional factors involved rather than focusing on abstract concepts of resistance.

"It sounds like you want to make this change and you also have concerns about making this change. Let's look at both sides specifically. What are the concrete benefits you expect if you make this change? What are the specific problems or costs you're worried about?"

Then: "Given both the benefits and the concerns, what information do you need to make a good decision? What would need to be different to tip the balance toward making this change?"

This approach treats ambivalence as a logical response to competing priorities rather than as a psychological barrier to overcome.

Marcus, a 31-year-old autistic accountant, seemed resistant to his therapist's suggestions about work-life balance. When they explored his concerns concretely, it became clear that he wasn't resistant to better work-life balance—he was concerned that leaving work earlier would result in incomplete tasks, which would cause him significant anxiety the next day. Together, they developed specific strategies for task completion and transition routines that addressed his actual concerns rather than trying to overcome abstract "resistance."

By speaking directly and concretely while maintaining warmth and respect, we create conditions for more effective communication with autistic individuals. The goal isn't to abandon empathy but to express empathy in ways that align with literal thinking styles.

The next chapter explores how to harness the intense interests that many autistic individuals have as powerful motivators for change, rather than viewing these interests as obstacles or distractions to therapy goals.

Essential takeaways

Literal language MI requires a fundamental shift in communication style without abandoning the collaborative, empathetic spirit of motivational interviewing. The key is recognizing that direct, concrete language often demonstrates more respect and care for autistic individuals than vague, metaphorical language that creates confusion and cognitive load.

Successful adaptation involves starting with concrete details and building toward abstract concepts, avoiding unhelpful metaphors, and providing clear operational definitions for therapeutic concepts. Most importantly, it means understanding that clarity and warmth aren't opposites—clear communication often feels more supportive and empathetic to people who think literally.

This approach benefits many neurotypical individuals as well, as concrete language and specific examples often enhance understanding and engagement across different thinking styles.

Chapter 5: Special Interests as Motivators

Leveraging focused passions

When Dr. Rodriguez first met 19-year-old Caleb, she noticed his desk was covered with train schedules, model locomotives, and railway maps from around the world. Caleb had come to therapy because his parents were concerned about his "obsession" with trains interfering with his college performance and social relationships.

Dr. Rodriguez's initial instinct was to help Caleb reduce his focus on trains so he could better attend to other life areas. But as she learned more about motivational interviewing approaches for autism, she realized she was looking at this completely backward.

Caleb's intense interest in trains wasn't a problem to solve—it was a powerful motivational resource to leverage.

Over the following months, Caleb used his train expertise to develop organizational systems based on railway scheduling principles. He connected with other train enthusiasts online, developing social skills through shared interests. He even changed his major to transportation engineering, transforming his "obsessive" interest into career preparation.

The shift in perspective changed everything. Instead of trying to reduce Caleb's passion for trains, Dr. Rodriguez learned to work with this intense interest as a strength and motivational foundation.

Identifying and incorporating special interests

Special interests—intense, focused passions that many autistic individuals develop—are often misunderstood in therapeutic contexts. Traditional approaches frequently view these interests as obstacles to "normal" functioning or as symptoms to manage rather than recognizing them as potential strengths and motivational resources.

Research indicates that **85-95% of autistic individuals have special interests**, and these interests often provide significant emotional regulation, social connection, and cognitive engagement benefits (Charlop-Christy & Haymes, 1996). Rather than pathologizing or minimizing these interests, effective MI with autistic individuals leverages them strategically.

Understanding the intensity and function of special interests

Special interests serve multiple important functions for autistic individuals beyond simple enjoyment or hobby engagement.

Emotional regulation: Engaging with special interests often provides comfort, reduces anxiety, and helps manage overwhelming emotions or sensory experiences.

Cognitive organization: Many autistic individuals use their special interests as frameworks for understanding and organizing information about the world.

Social connection: Special interests can provide pathways to meaningful relationships with others who share similar passions.

Identity and self-esteem: Areas of expertise and intense knowledge often contribute significantly to positive self-concept and confidence.

Sensory satisfaction: Many special interests involve preferred sensory experiences—the visual patterns of train schedules, the tactile experience of collecting objects, or the auditory satisfaction of music.

The assessment of special interests

Rather than asking generally about hobbies or interests, use specific questions that help identify the intensity, function, and scope of special interests.

"What topics or activities can you think about or engage with for hours without getting bored or tired?"

"When you're stressed or overwhelmed, what do you like to think about or do that helps you feel better?"

"What subjects do you know more about than most people around you?"

"If you had a completely free day with no obligations, how would you choose to spend your time?"

"What topics do you find yourself bringing up in conversations, even when others might not be as interested?"

Mapping interest characteristics

Once you identify special interests, explore their specific characteristics and how they currently function in the person's life.

Knowledge depth: How extensive is their knowledge in this area? Are they self-taught experts? Do they know historical details, technical specifications, or nuanced information that others wouldn't know?

Time investment: How much time do they naturally spend thinking about or engaging with this interest? How does this time distribution affect other life activities?

Social aspects: Do they engage with online communities, attend conventions, or connect with others who share this interest? Or is it primarily a solitary pursuit?

Creative expression: Do they create content, write, build, or produce things related to their interest? Do they have collections, artwork, or projects?

Learning patterns: How do they acquire new information about their interest? Do they read extensively, watch videos, attend events, or experiment hands-on?

Emma, a 26-year-old autistic woman, has an intense interest in medieval history. She's read hundreds of books on the topic, participates in online forums, attends Renaissance faires, and has taught herself blacksmithing and historically accurate cooking techniques. When her therapist asked about this interest, Emma's entire demeanor changed—she became more animated, spoke with greater confidence, and demonstrated remarkable knowledge depth and enthusiasm.

Using intense interests to build motivation for change

The key insight is that special interests aren't competing with therapeutic goals—they can be powerful vehicles for achieving therapeutic goals. Instead of asking people to spend less time on their interests so they can work on other life areas, explore how their interests can support growth in those other areas.

Interest-based goal development

Start with the person's natural motivation and energy around their special interests, then explore connections to broader life goals.

"You clearly have incredible expertise and passion around [special interest]. How could we use that expertise to help with [therapeutic goal]?"

"When you're engaged with [special interest], you show amazing focus, persistence, and problem-solving skills. How could we apply those same strengths to [life challenge]?"

Practical examples:

Organization and time management: Someone interested in sports statistics might develop personal organization systems based on statistical tracking and analysis methods.

Social skills development: Someone passionate about anime might develop social connections through fan communities, conventions, or online discussions, building confidence that transfers to other social situations.

Career development: Someone fascinated by marine biology might pursue education or volunteer opportunities in environmental science, aquariums, or conservation work.

Self-advocacy skills: Someone with deep knowledge about their interest area can practice explaining complex topics to others, building communication skills that apply to self-advocacy in other contexts.

Motivation transfer techniques

Help people recognize the motivational and skill patterns that show up in their special interests and apply those same patterns to other life areas.

"When you're learning about [special interest], you're incredibly persistent and will spend hours researching until you understand something completely. That's a remarkable strength. What would it look like to apply that same persistence to [other goal]?"

"I notice that you have systems for organizing your [special interest collection/information]. You know exactly where everything is and how it all connects. How could we create similar organizational systems for [other life area]?"

David has an intense interest in computer programming and can spend hours debugging code without frustration. His therapist helped him recognize that this persistence and systematic problem-solving approach could apply to social challenges: "You approach coding problems by breaking them down into smaller components, testing different solutions systematically, and not getting discouraged when the first approach doesn't work. How could you apply that same systematic approach to developing social connections?"

Energy and engagement leverage

Special interests represent areas where people have natural energy, focus, and sustained attention. Use these as starting points for building momentum toward other goals rather than fighting against them.

Schedule challenging tasks immediately before or after special interest time: The positive emotional state and mental energy from engaging with interests can provide momentum for more difficult activities.

Use special interest time as rewards: Instead of viewing special interest engagement as "wasted time," frame it as earned reward time that motivates completion of other important tasks.

Connect routine activities to special interests: Find ways to incorporate elements of special interests into daily necessary activities to increase engagement and reduce resistance.

Maria loves everything about cats—cat behavior, genetics, breeds, history, and care. She struggled with maintaining her living space because cleaning felt boring and overwhelming. Her therapist helped her reframe household maintenance through her cat interest: she researched how different cleaning products affect cats, created a cleaning schedule based on optimal feline environmental health, and even got houseplants that are safe for cats and improve air quality. Her living space improved dramatically because the tasks felt connected to something she genuinely cared about.

Connecting change goals to areas of expertise

One of the most powerful motivational strategies is helping people apply their expertise from special interest areas to other life challenges. This approach leverages their natural confidence, knowledge, and problem-solving abilities while honoring their areas of strength.

The expert consultation approach

Position the person as an expert consultant applying their knowledge to solve problems in other life domains.

"You know more about [special interest] than anyone I've ever met. If someone came to you with a problem in that area, you'd be able to help them figure out solutions. Let's approach [life challenge] the same way—as a problem that your expertise and problem-solving skills can help solve."

This reframes therapeutic work from "fixing deficits" to "applying strengths," which often feels more empowering and engaging for autistic individuals.

Problem-solving methodology transfer

Help people identify the systematic approaches they use in their special interest areas and apply those same methodologies to other challenges.

Research and information gathering: "When you want to understand something about [special interest], how do you go about learning? What sources do you trust? How do you evaluate conflicting information? Could we use that same approach to learn about [life challenge]?"

Systematic analysis: "When you're trying to solve a problem related to [special interest], what steps do you take? How do you break down complex problems into manageable pieces? Let's use that same systematic approach for [current challenge]."

Quality standards: "You have incredibly high standards for accuracy and completeness when it comes to [special interest]. How could we apply those same quality standards to [other goal]?"

Ben is passionate about astronomy and has extensive knowledge about celestial mechanics, telescope operations, and astrophotography. He struggled with financial planning because it felt overwhelming and boring. His therapist helped him approach financial planning like an astronomy project: he researched different investment options with the same thoroughness he used to research telescopes, created spreadsheets to track financial data like he tracked celestial observations, and set long-term financial goals with the same patience he used for multi-year astrophotography projects.

Knowledge application exercises

Create specific exercises that allow people to apply their special interest knowledge to broader life skills.

Teaching and explanation practice: Ask them to explain complex aspects of their special interest to you, building communication and social skills that transfer to other contexts.

Comparison and analogy creation: Help them find parallels between their special interest knowledge and other life situations, building abstract thinking and problem-solving flexibility.

System design challenges: If they understand complex systems in their interest area, challenge them to design systems for other life areas using similar principles.

Confidence building through expertise

Special interests represent areas where autistic individuals often experience competence, mastery, and confidence—feelings that may be less common in other life areas. Use this foundation of positive self-concept to build confidence for approaching new challenges.

"When you talk about [special interest], I can see your expertise and confidence. You know you're capable of mastering complex information and solving difficult problems. That same intelligence and capability that you apply to [special interest] is available to help you with [other challenge]."

Maintaining balance between interests and broader goals

While special interests can be powerful motivational tools, it's important to help people maintain balance and ensure that interest-focused time doesn't completely crowd out attention to other important life areas. The goal isn't to reduce special interests but to find sustainable ways to honor both passionate interests and broader life functioning.

Collaborative time management

Work with people to create schedules that honor both their need for special interest engagement and their goals in other life areas.

"How much time with [special interest] do you need to feel satisfied and emotionally regulated? What's the minimum amount of time that would feel restrictive or stressful?"

"What other life areas need attention for you to feel functional and satisfied overall? How much time do those areas realistically require?"

"How can we create a schedule that honors both your passion for [special interest] and your goals in [other areas]?"

Create collaborative rather than restrictive approaches: Instead of "You can only spend one hour per day on trains," try "You want to spend time with trains and also work on your college courses. How can we structure your week so you have satisfying time for both?"

Interest-integrated life planning

Rather than compartmentalizing special interests separately from "real life," explore ways to integrate them into broader life planning.

Career connections: Are there career paths that incorporate their special interests? Educational programs? Volunteer opportunities? Professional communities?

Social connections: How can their special interests connect them with like-minded people and meaningful relationships?

Creative expression: How can their interests contribute to creative fulfillment, artistic expression, or meaningful projects?

Life contribution: How can their expertise benefit others or contribute to their community?

Rachel has an intense interest in birds—identification, behavior, migration patterns, and conservation. Instead of viewing this as separate from her "real" career goals, her therapist helped her explore connections: she volunteered with local bird conservation groups, which led to networking opportunities in environmental science; she started a bird-watching blog that developed her writing skills; she took photography classes to improve her bird photography, which became a source of income; and she eventually found work with a nonprofit focused on habitat preservation.

Flexibility and life stage considerations

Special interests may need different integration approaches during different life stages or circumstances. Help people develop flexible approaches that can adapt to changing life demands.

High-demand periods: During college finals, work deadlines, or family crises, how can they maintain some special interest engagement without compromising other essential activities?

Low-demand periods: During vacations, breaks, or less structured times, how can they fully enjoy their interests without losing momentum in other areas?

Life transitions: When starting new jobs, relationships, or living situations, how can they maintain their interests while adapting to new demands?

The sustainability check

Regularly assess whether the current balance between special interests and other life areas feels sustainable and satisfying.

"How is the current balance working for you? Do you feel like you're getting enough time with [special interest] to feel satisfied? Are other life areas getting enough attention to function well?"

"What adjustments would make this balance work better? What would need to change for you to feel more satisfied overall?"

"Are there areas where your interest in [special topic] is helping with other life goals? Are there areas where it might be creating challenges we should address?"

Supporting interest evolution

Special interests sometimes change, evolve, or expand over time. Support people in adapting their life integration as their interests develop.

"I've noticed you're becoming interested in [new area] in addition to [original interest]. How do these interests relate to each other? How might this affect your goals and plans?"

"Your interest in [topic] seems to be expanding into [related area]. What opportunities might that create? What adjustments might be helpful?"

Special interests aren't obstacles to overcome or distractions to manage—they're powerful resources for motivation, learning, and personal growth. When we learn to work with these intense passions rather than against them, we often find that autistic individuals have remarkable capacities for persistence, expertise development, and creative problem-solving that can be applied across many life areas.

The next chapter explores the unique challenges that social communication differences create in change conversations and

how to adapt MI approaches for different social contexts and relationship goals.

Working with what works

Special interests represent some of the strongest natural motivation and engagement that autistic individuals experience. Rather than viewing these intense passions as problems to manage or obstacles to overcome, effective MI leverages them as powerful resources for personal growth and life satisfaction.

The key insight is that the same qualities that fuel special interests—persistence, attention to detail, deep learning, and sustained engagement—can be redirected toward other life goals when we create appropriate connections and applications. This approach honors autistic individuals' natural strengths while supporting their broader life functioning.

This strength-based perspective often reveals remarkable capabilities and resources that might otherwise remain hidden or underutilized in traditional deficit-focused therapeutic approaches.

Chapter 6: Social Navigation

Change talk in relationship contexts

Lisa, a 23-year-old autistic college student, sat in her therapist's office expressing frustration about her social life. "I want better relationships," she said, "but I don't understand what I'm doing wrong. People seem to lose interest in being friends with me, and I can't figure out why."

Her therapist, Dr. Kumar, had been trained in traditional MI approaches that assume people naturally understand social dynamics and can identify relationship patterns through self-reflection. But Lisa's challenges weren't about lack of motivation or ambivalence about relationships—they were about navigating the complex, often unspoken rules of social interaction that neurotypical people learn intuitively but that can feel like an incomprehensible foreign language to autistic individuals.

Dr. Kumar realized that addressing Lisa's relationship goals required understanding the unique social communication differences that affect how autistic people experience and navigate social connections. Traditional MI approaches to relationship issues needed significant adaptation to work effectively.

Understanding social communication differences

Autistic individuals often experience social communication in fundamentally different ways than neurotypical people. These differences aren't deficits or social skills "problems" to fix—they're neurological variations that require different approaches to social connection and relationship building.

Research indicates that **social communication challenges affect over 90% of autistic individuals**, but these challenges often stem from differences in social processing rather than lack of social motivation (American Psychiatric Association, 2013). Many autistic people genuinely want social connections but struggle with the unspoken rules and expectations of neurotypical social interaction.

Processing social information differently

Neurotypical social communication relies heavily on nonverbal cues, implied meanings, social context, and unspoken rules that many autistic individuals find difficult to interpret or remember to use.

Nonverbal communication challenges: Reading facial expressions, interpreting tone of voice, understanding personal space boundaries, and using appropriate eye contact don't come naturally to many autistic people. They might miss social cues that neurotypical people consider obvious or important.

Literal interpretation: Sarcasm, jokes, indirect requests, and implied meanings can be confusing or misunderstood. When someone says "Nice weather we're having" during a thunderstorm, an autistic person might genuinely discuss the weather rather than recognizing sarcasm.

Social context switching: Understanding that the same behavior might be appropriate in one social context but inappropriate in another requires flexible thinking that can be challenging. Talking enthusiastically about special interests might be welcome at a fan convention but overwhelming on a first date.

Turn-taking and reciprocity: The natural rhythm of conversation—knowing when to speak, how long to talk, when to ask questions about others—often needs to be explicitly learned rather than intuitively understood.

Executive function impacts on social interaction

Social interaction places significant demands on executive functioning—the brain's management system for planning, attention, and behavioral regulation. For autistic individuals who already experience executive function challenges, social situations can be particularly exhausting.

Social planning: Determining appropriate topics, remembering social rules, monitoring the other person's reactions, and adjusting behavior accordingly all require significant mental energy and attention.

Simultaneous processing demands: In social interactions, autistic individuals might be working to: process what the other person is saying, interpret their nonverbal cues, plan their own response, monitor their own behavior, remember social rules, and manage sensory input from the environment.

Social fatigue: The cognitive load of social interaction can be exhausting, leading to what many autistic people describe as "social burnout" where they need significant alone time to recover.

Sensory factors in social situations

Social environments often include significant sensory challenges that can interfere with an autistic person's ability to engage socially.

Overwhelming environments: Restaurants, parties, group gatherings, and other social venues often involve bright lights, loud conversations, background music, strong smells, and crowded spaces that can be sensory overwhelming.

Competing attention demands: When an autistic person is managing sensory overwhelm, they have less cognitive capacity available for social processing and interaction.

Sensory-seeking behaviors: Stimming, fidgeting, or other self-regulation behaviors that help manage sensory input might be misinterpreted by others as disinterest or rudeness.

Different social motivations and preferences

Autistic individuals often have genuine interest in social connection but may prefer different types of social interaction than neurotypical people expect.

Deep vs. broad social connections: Many autistic people prefer fewer, deeper relationships rather than large social circles with casual acquaintances.

Shared interest connections: Relationships built around shared interests or activities might feel more comfortable and sustainable than relationships focused primarily on social chat or emotional sharing.

Parallel social activities: Some autistic individuals prefer "parallel play" types of social connection—being near others while engaged in individual activities—rather than direct face-to-face conversation.

Online vs. in-person interaction: Digital communication can be easier because it removes nonverbal communication demands and allows for processing time before responding.

MI in one-on-one vs. group settings

The social demands of different therapeutic settings significantly affect how autistic individuals can engage in motivational interviewing conversations. Understanding these differences allows for more effective therapeutic planning and intervention.

One-on-one advantages for autistic clients

Individual MI sessions offer several advantages that align with autistic communication preferences and processing styles.

Reduced social complexity: With only one other person, there are fewer social cues to monitor, fewer conversational dynamics to track, and more predictable interaction patterns.

Personalized pacing: The therapist can adjust conversation speed, processing time, and topic transitions to match the individual's specific needs without considering group dynamics.

Special interest integration: Discussions can incorporate the person's special interests without concern about boring or excluding others.

Sensory control: Environmental factors can be optimized for the individual's sensory needs without compromising group members' comfort.

Direct communication: Clear, literal language and explicit structure can be used without worrying about how it affects group process.

One-on-one MI adaptations

Maximize the advantages of individual therapy by adapting MI techniques specifically for autistic social communication patterns.

Explicit social contracting: "In our sessions, you don't need to maintain eye contact, you can fidget or move if it helps you think, and you can take as much time as you need to process questions. I'll be direct in my communication and ask for clarification if I don't understand something. How does that sound?"

Interest-based rapport building: Instead of traditional small talk, build connection through genuine curiosity about their interests and expertise. "I'd love to learn more about [their special interest]. Can you tell me what got you interested in that topic?"

Structured social skill practice: Use the therapeutic relationship as a safe space to practice social communication skills. "Some people find it helpful to practice having conversations about difficult topics in therapy before having them in other relationships. Would that be useful for you?"

Meta-social discussions: Talk explicitly about social dynamics, relationship patterns, and communication challenges. "You mentioned that friendships often fade after a few months. Have you noticed any patterns in how that happens?"

Group setting challenges

Group therapy or MI sessions present additional social complexity that can be overwhelming for autistic individuals.

Multiple social dynamics: Tracking multiple people's nonverbal cues, conversation contributions, and emotional states simultaneously can be cognitively exhausting.

Unpredictable social flow: Group conversations change direction rapidly, topics shift unexpectedly, and multiple people might speak at once or interrupt each other.

Performance anxiety: Concern about saying the "wrong" thing or appearing different can increase anxiety and reduce authentic engagement.

Masking pressure: Group settings often increase pressure to appear neurotypical, which is exhausting and can interfere with genuine therapeutic work.

Sensory overwhelm: More people means more sensory input—more voices, movement, smells, and environmental stimulation.

Adapting group MI for autistic participants

When group settings are necessary or beneficial, specific adaptations can increase accessibility and effectiveness.

Smaller groups: Limit group size to 3-4 people rather than larger groups to reduce social complexity.

Structured interaction: Provide clear guidelines about turn-taking, topic focus, and time limits to reduce unpredictability.

Written agendas: Give participants advance notice about topics and structure so they can prepare mentally.

Sensory accommodations: Ensure lighting, seating, and environmental factors work for participants' sensory needs.

Break options: Allow people to step out or take breaks without penalty if they become overwhelmed.

Interest-based groups: Consider forming groups around shared interests rather than diagnostic categories or general social skills.

Mixed neurotype group considerations

Groups that include both autistic and neurotypical participants require careful attention to communication style differences.

Communication norms: Establish explicit group norms that accommodate both direct autistic communication styles and neurotypical indirect communication preferences.

Pace variations: Some group members may need more processing time while others prefer faster-paced interaction. Build in structured pauses and varied interaction formats.

Interest sharing: Create opportunities for people to share their areas of expertise and passion without dominating the conversation.

Social interpretation support: When miscommunication occurs, help group members understand different communication styles rather than assuming intent or rudeness.

Supporting social change goals

When autistic individuals express goals related to improving relationships or social connections, it's important to understand what they mean specifically and help them develop realistic, personalized approaches to social growth.

Clarifying social goals

Abstract relationship goals need to be translated into specific, concrete objectives that align with autistic social preferences and capabilities.

"I want to be more social" might mean:

- "I want one close friend I can talk to regularly"
- "I want to feel more comfortable in group situations at work"

- "I want to find people who share my interests"

- "I want to understand social rules better so I make fewer mistakes"

- "I want romantic relationship skills"

- "I want to feel less lonely"

Explore specific social desires: "When you say you want better relationships, what would that look like specifically? What would be different about your daily or weekly life? What kinds of interactions would you have more of or less of?"

"Think about a social interaction you've had that felt good to you. What made it work well? What would you like to have more of like that?"

Strength-based social skill development

Rather than focusing on social deficits, identify and build on existing social strengths and preferences.

Communication strengths: Many autistic individuals are excellent listeners, have strong loyalty to friends, are reliable and honest, and bring unique perspectives to relationships.

Interest-based connections: Help people identify communities, groups, or activities where their special interests create natural connection points with others.

One-on-one relationship skills: Many autistic people excel in deeper, individual relationships even if they struggle with group dynamics.

Digital communication: Online communities, text-based communication, or video calls might be easier starting points for social connection.

Practical social support: Some autistic individuals are excellent at providing practical help, problem-solving, or task-oriented support in relationships.

Realistic relationship expectations

Help people develop realistic expectations about relationships that honor both their social goals and their neurological realities.

Quality over quantity: Most autistic people benefit from focusing on developing fewer, deeper relationships rather than trying to maintain large social circles.

Energy management: Social relationships require energy investment. Help people plan for social activities and build in recovery time.

Communication style matching: Relationships work best when communication styles are compatible or when there's mutual understanding of different styles.

Interest compatibility: Relationships built around shared interests or values tend to be more sustainable than those based solely on social compatibility.

Accommodation needs: Healthy relationships for autistic people often require partners who can accommodate sensory needs, communication differences, and social preferences.

Social skill practice in therapeutic contexts

Use the therapeutic relationship as a safe laboratory for practicing and developing social skills.

Direct feedback: "I noticed when you told me about your weekend, you gave me a lot of technical details but didn't mention how you felt about the activities. Some people connect through sharing emotions and reactions. Would you like to practice including more of your personal experience in storytelling?"

Social interpretation practice: "When your coworker said [example], what did you think they meant? Let's explore different possible interpretations and how you might respond to each."

Conversation skills: Practice specific conversation techniques like asking follow-up questions, sharing appropriate personal information, or transitioning between topics smoothly.

Conflict resolution: Develop scripts and strategies for addressing misunderstandings, setting boundaries, or navigating disagreements.

Family and peer relationship considerations

Autistic individuals often face unique challenges in family and peer relationships that require specialized MI approaches addressing both individual growth and systemic relationship dynamics.

Family system understanding

Families of autistic individuals often develop complex dynamics around communication, expectations, and support that need to be understood and addressed in therapeutic work.

Communication patterns: Family members may have developed patterns of interpreting for the autistic person, making decisions for them, or having different communication rules than the outside world uses.

Expectation conflicts: Parents or siblings might have neurotypical expectations for social behavior that create tension or pressure for the autistic family member.

Support vs. independence: Families often struggle with balancing support for autistic family members with encouraging independence and autonomy.

Masking within families: Some autistic individuals work hard to appear neurotypical within their families, creating exhaustion and authenticity challenges.

Family-inclusive MI approaches

Consider involving family members in MI conversations when appropriate and when the autistic person consents.

Education and understanding: Help family members understand autistic communication patterns and social needs so they can provide more effective support.

Communication coaching: Work with families to develop communication approaches that work for the autistic person's processing style.

Boundary setting: Support autistic individuals in communicating their needs and boundaries to family members clearly and directly.

Expectation adjustment: Help families develop realistic expectations that honor both the autistic person's neurology and their growth potential.

Peer relationship navigation

Peer relationships often present different challenges than family relationships and require different skill sets and strategies.

Workplace relationships: Professional relationships have different demands and expectations than personal friendships, requiring specific skills and approaches.

Romantic relationships: Dating and intimate relationships require navigation of complex social and emotional dynamics that may need explicit exploration and skill development.

Friend maintenance: Understanding how to maintain friendships over time, handle conflict, and balance different friends' needs requires ongoing skill development.

Community involvement: Participating in community groups, religious organizations, or hobby communities creates opportunities for connection but also requires social navigation skills.

Addressing social rejection and isolation

Many autistic individuals have experienced social rejection, bullying, or isolation that affects their willingness to pursue relationships and their confidence in social situations.

Trauma-informed approaches: Past negative social experiences may create anxiety, avoidance, or hypervigilance in social situations that needs therapeutic attention.

Self-advocacy development: Building skills for communicating needs, setting boundaries, and advocating for accommodations in relationships.

Resilience building: Developing strategies for managing social rejection, misunderstandings, or relationship conflicts without abandoning social goals entirely.

Support network development: Helping people identify and connect with communities that are autism-friendly and accepting of neurodivergent communication styles.

Social navigation for autistic individuals requires a nuanced understanding of both their genuine social motivations and the unique challenges they face in neurotypical social environments. The goal isn't to make autistic people more neurotypical in their social approach but to help them develop authentic, sustainable relationships that honor their neurological reality while meeting their connection needs.

The next chapter addresses one of the most significant challenges in working with autistic individuals around change: understanding and working with their need for routine and predictability when change inherently disrupts these important regulatory systems.

Building authentic connections

Social challenges for autistic individuals stem from the mismatch between neurotypical social expectations and autistic communication patterns, not from lack of social motivation or ability. Effective MI approaches honor these differences while supporting genuine relationship goals.

The key insight is that autistic individuals often have strong desires for social connection but may need different types of relationships and social interactions than neurotypical people prefer. By understanding these differences and building on autistic strengths in communication and connection, we can support meaningful relationship development that feels authentic and sustainable.

This requires moving beyond deficit-focused social skills training toward strength-based approaches that honor autistic ways of connecting while building skills for navigating neurotypical social environments when necessary.

Chapter 7: Routine Disruption

Managing transition resistance

When 32-year-old Michael's therapist suggested he might benefit from changing his morning routine to include exercise, Michael's reaction was immediate and intense. His shoulders tensed, his voice became strained, and he said, "I can't change my morning routine. I've been doing the same routine for eight years. If I change it, my whole day falls apart."

The therapist, Dr. Park, initially interpreted this as resistance to change or perhaps laziness regarding exercise. But as she learned more about autism and routine needs, she realized that Michael's response wasn't about being stubborn or unmotivated. **His morning routine served as a crucial regulatory system that helped organize his thinking, manage anxiety, and prepare him to handle the unpredictable demands of his day.**

Suggesting he change this routine was like asking someone to remove a load-bearing wall from their house and hoping the structure would remain stable.

Dr. Park learned that working with autistic individuals around change requires understanding why routines are so important and developing approaches that honor these needs while still supporting growth and adaptation.

Why change feels threatening to autistic individuals

For many autistic people, routines and predictability aren't just preferences—they're neurological necessities that support cognitive functioning, emotional regulation, and daily life management. Understanding this difference is crucial for anyone attempting to support change in autistic individuals' lives.

Cognitive load and executive function support

Routines significantly reduce the cognitive load required for daily functioning. When activities follow predictable patterns, less mental energy is needed for planning, decision-making, and behavioral regulation, freeing up cognitive capacity for other tasks.

Decision fatigue reduction: Having established routines means fewer decisions to make throughout the day. Michael doesn't have to decide what to eat for breakfast, what order to do his morning activities, or what to wear—these decisions are already made by his routine structure.

Executive function scaffolding: Routines provide external structure that supports executive functioning. The routine itself serves as a planning system, attention guide, and behavioral prompt.

Cognitive predictability: Knowing what comes next reduces anxiety and allows the brain to prepare for upcoming activities rather than constantly scanning for what might happen.

Sensory regulation through predictability

Routines often include sensory elements that support regulation and comfort. Changes to routines can disrupt carefully balanced sensory input that helps maintain optimal arousal levels.

Sensory scheduling: Many autistic individuals unconsciously build sensory regulation into their routines—quiet time in the morning, specific foods with preferred textures, familiar music, or predictable physical activities.

Arousal level management: Routines help maintain appropriate arousal levels throughout the day by providing the right amount of stimulation or calm at different times.

Sensory preparation: Knowing what sensory experiences to expect allows the nervous system to prepare rather than being constantly reactive to unexpected input.

Emotional regulation and anxiety management

Predictable routines provide emotional stability and reduce anxiety about uncertainty. For many autistic individuals, routine disruption can trigger significant distress that goes far beyond simple annoyance.

Anxiety prevention: Routines reduce the uncertainty that often triggers anxiety in autistic individuals. When someone knows what to expect, their nervous system can remain calmer.

Emotional preparation: Predictable sequences allow people to prepare emotionally for different parts of their day, transitioning gradually between activities and mental states.

Safety and comfort: Familiar routines create psychological safety and comfort, providing a stable foundation that supports engaging with less predictable aspects of life.

Identity and competence maintenance

For many autistic people, routines represent areas of competence and control in a world that often feels chaotic or demanding.

Mastery and expertise: People often become very skilled at their established routines, knowing exactly how long tasks take, what works best, and how to optimize their approaches.

Autonomy and control: In a world where autistic individuals often feel pressure to conform to neurotypical expectations, routines can represent areas of personal autonomy and self-determination.

Identity expression: Routines sometimes incorporate special interests, values, or personal preferences in ways that feel authentic and self-expressive.

Gradual transition strategies

Effective change approaches for autistic individuals work with their need for predictability rather than against it. Instead of expecting people to abandon helpful routines, successful strategies gradually modify routines while maintaining their regulatory benefits.

The routine analysis approach

Before suggesting changes to any routine, understand its current function and importance.

Functional assessment: "Help me understand your morning routine. Walk me through exactly what you do and when you do it. Which parts feel most important to you? Which parts would be hardest to change?"

Benefit identification: "What does your routine do for you? How does it help your day go well? What would be different about your day if this routine didn't exist?"

Flexibility points: "Are there any parts of your routine that already vary sometimes? Are there steps that feel more flexible or less important than others?"

Timing analysis: "How much time does your routine take? Are there time pressures or scheduling constraints we need to consider?"

Micro-change integration

Instead of major routine overhauls, introduce tiny modifications that maintain the routine's essential structure while gradually incorporating desired changes.

Single element modification: Change only one small element at a time while keeping everything else exactly the same. Michael might keep his entire morning routine identical but add two minutes of stretching between existing activities.

Addition rather than replacement: Instead of replacing routine elements, add new elements to existing structure. Rather than

78

changing breakfast, add a five-minute walk after the current breakfast routine.

Time shifting: Move routine elements to different times rather than eliminating them. If someone wants to add evening exercise but has important evening routines, consider moving some evening activities to morning to create space.

Sequential integration: Introduce changes in predictable sequences so they become part of the routine structure rather than disruptions to it.

The parallel routine approach

Develop new routines alongside existing ones rather than replacing established patterns immediately.

Weekend vs. weekday routines: Experiment with changes during weekends or days off when disruption has less impact on important functioning.

Alternative situation routines: Create different routines for different circumstances (travel routines, sick day routines, holiday routines) that maintain structure while allowing for variation.

Backup routine development: Develop secondary routines that can be used when primary routines aren't possible, maintaining predictability even when circumstances change.

Seasonal routine variation: Gradually modify routines to align with seasonal changes or life transitions while maintaining core structural elements.

Change rehearsal and mental preparation

Help people prepare mentally for routine changes through visualization, planning, and gradual exposure.

Detailed planning: Work through exactly how the modified routine will look, addressing potential challenges and decision points in advance.

Mental rehearsal: Practice the new routine mentally before implementing it physically, reducing uncertainty and building familiarity.

Contingency planning: Identify what to do if the new routine doesn't work as expected, providing backup plans that reduce anxiety about change.

Gradual exposure: Introduce small elements of change in low-stakes situations before implementing them in important daily routines.

Maintaining predictability within change processes

The goal isn't to eliminate predictability but to create predictable change processes that honor the need for structure while supporting adaptation and growth.

Structured change frameworks

Develop consistent approaches to change that become predictable in themselves.

Change process routines: Create standard procedures for how changes will be introduced, evaluated, and modified. "Whenever we consider changing part of your routine, we'll first analyze how it currently works, then identify one small modification, then try it for one week, then evaluate how it went."

Regular review schedules: Establish predictable times for reviewing and adjusting routines rather than making changes randomly or reactively.

Communication protocols: Develop standard ways of discussing potential changes, ensuring the person has adequate information and input before changes are implemented.

Documentation systems: Keep records of what changes work, what doesn't work, and what factors influence success, creating a knowledge base for future modifications.

Predictable flexibility development

Help people develop flexibility skills in structured, predictable ways rather than expecting spontaneous adaptability.

Flexibility practice: Create low-stakes opportunities to practice handling small changes or disruptions in routine, building tolerance gradually.

Alternative option development: For important routine elements, develop two or three acceptable alternatives so choice exists within predictable parameters.

Disruption planning: Prepare in advance for predictable disruptions (schedule changes, travel, illness) by planning alternative routines for these situations.

Recovery routines: Develop standard procedures for returning to preferred routines after periods of necessary disruption.

Communication about change needs

Establish clear communication patterns around change that reduce uncertainty and honor the person's need for information and control.

Advance notice: Provide as much advance warning as possible about potential changes, allowing time for mental preparation and planning.

Choice preservation: Whenever possible, offer choices within change rather than imposing single solutions. "We need to modify this routine to accommodate your new work schedule. Here are three ways we could approach that. Which feels most workable to you?"

Rationale explanation: Clearly explain why changes are necessary or beneficial, providing logical reasoning that makes sense to concrete thinking patterns.

Timeline clarity: Be specific about when changes will be implemented, how long trial periods will last, and when modifications will be evaluated.

Supporting routine flexibility development

The ultimate goal is helping autistic individuals develop sustainable flexibility skills that allow for adaptation when necessary while maintaining the regulatory benefits of routine and predictability.

Graduated flexibility training

Build flexibility systematically through progressively more challenging variations within safe, supportive contexts.

Micro-variations: Start with tiny, temporary changes to non-essential routine elements. Change the brand of cereal occasionally or take a slightly different route to familiar destinations.

Choice-based variations: Introduce variations that the person controls and chooses rather than unexpected disruptions. "Today you can choose to do A, B, or C for this part of your routine."

Temporary disruptions: Practice handling short-term routine disruptions with planned return to normal patterns. "We're going to try this different approach for three days, then go back to your regular routine."

Situational adaptations: Develop flexibility skills for specific situations (travel, schedule changes, equipment problems) while maintaining routine stability in other areas.

Flexibility skill building

Teach specific cognitive and behavioral strategies for managing routine disruptions when they occur.

Problem-solving frameworks: Develop standard approaches for handling unexpected changes or disruptions to routine. "When something disrupts my routine, I will: assess what's different, identify what I can control, make temporary adjustments, and plan how to return to my preferred pattern."

Stress management techniques: Build skills for managing the anxiety and distress that routine disruption often causes, including sensory regulation strategies and emotional coping techniques.

Adaptation strategies: Develop specific techniques for modifying routines temporarily while maintaining their essential regulatory functions.

Communication skills: Build abilities to advocate for routine needs and negotiate accommodations in situations where flexibility is required.

Environmental support for flexibility

Create environmental conditions that support flexibility development while honoring the need for predictability.

Supportive relationships: Work with family members, friends, and colleagues to understand routine needs and provide appropriate support during changes.

Accommodation planning: Develop workplace, school, or home accommodations that reduce unnecessary routine disruptions while building skills for handling necessary changes.

Resource development: Create tools, systems, and supports that make routine modifications easier and less stressful.

Community building: Connect with other autistic individuals and supportive communities that understand and respect routine needs while encouraging appropriate growth.

Sarah, a 29-year-old autistic accountant, worked with her therapist to gradually build flexibility around her work routines. They started by identifying which parts of her work routine were essential for functioning (specific organizational systems, timing of complex tasks, sensory break schedules) and which parts had potential flexibility (lunch timing, meeting locations, project sequencing). Over several months, Sarah practiced small variations in the flexible areas while maintaining stability in essential areas. When her department restructured and her routine had to change significantly, Sarah had developed enough flexibility skills to adapt successfully while advocating for the accommodations she needed to maintain her essential regulatory routines.

The key insight is that routine flexibility for autistic individuals doesn't mean abandoning structure—it means developing more sophisticated and adaptable structures that can bend without breaking. When we honor the regulatory function of routines while gradually building flexibility skills, autistic individuals can develop impressive capacities for adaptation while maintaining their neurological needs for predictability and control.

This completes Part II of our exploration of autism-specific adaptations to motivational interviewing. The next section will focus on ADHD applications, beginning with how dopamine-driven motivation systems require completely different approaches to change conversations than traditional MI assumes.

Understanding routine as foundation

Routine resistance in autistic individuals isn't stubbornness or inflexibility—it's a neurological need for predictability that supports cognitive functioning, emotional regulation, and daily life management. Effective change approaches work with this need rather than against it.

The most successful strategies gradually modify routines while maintaining their regulatory benefits, develop predictable change processes, and build flexibility skills systematically rather than expecting spontaneous adaptability. This honors both the person's neurological needs and their potential for growth and adaptation.

When we understand routines as sophisticated regulatory systems rather than rigid limitations, we can support meaningful change that feels sustainable and empowering rather than threatening and overwhelming.

Chapter 8: Dopamine-Driven Conversations

Working with reward systems

Jake sat across from his counselor, bouncing his leg rapidly under the table. His counselor had just asked him about his goals for therapy, and Jake's response tumbled out in a rapid stream: "I want to finish my degree, but I keep starting projects and not finishing them, and I know I should exercise but it's so boring, and I really need to organize my apartment but every time I start I get distracted by something more interesting, and I feel like such a failure because everyone else seems to be able to just decide to do things and then do them."

His counselor, trained in traditional motivational interviewing, began exploring Jake's ambivalence about these goals. But what she didn't understand was that Jake wasn't ambivalent—he was experiencing the classic ADHD motivation paradox. **His brain craved dopamine stimulation to function properly, but most of his important goals were inherently low-dopamine activities that his reward system simply couldn't sustain.**

Jake's rapid leg bouncing wasn't anxiety or restlessness—it was his brain's attempt to generate the stimulation needed to maintain attention during their conversation. The real challenge wasn't identifying what Jake wanted to change. It was figuring out how to work with his dopamine-driven neurology to make change sustainable.

Understanding ADHD motivation and dopamine

ADHD fundamentally affects the brain's reward and motivation systems through dysregulated dopamine function. Traditional motivational interviewing assumes that people can sustain motivation for important goals through willpower, planning, and commitment. For individuals with ADHD, this assumption breaks down because their brains require different kinds of motivational fuel to maintain engagement and follow-through.

The dopamine deficit reality

Research consistently shows that ADHD involves dysregulation in dopamine pathways, particularly in areas of the brain responsible for motivation, reward processing, and executive function (Volkow et al., 2009). This isn't a character flaw or lack of willpower—it's a neurochemical reality that affects how ADHD brains respond to different types of tasks and rewards.

Baseline dopamine differences: ADHD brains often have lower baseline dopamine activity, meaning they require more stimulation to reach optimal functioning levels. What feels motivating to a neurotypical brain might not provide enough activation for an ADHD brain.

Reward sensitivity variations: Tasks that provide immediate, novel, or intense rewards capture ADHD attention easily, while tasks with delayed, predictable, or subtle rewards struggle to maintain engagement regardless of their importance.

Interest-driven hyperfocus: When ADHD brains encounter high-dopamine activities (novel, interesting, challenging, or personally meaningful), they can sustain attention for hours. This same brain that "can't focus" on boring but important tasks might spend six hours straight learning about a fascinating topic.

The neurotypical motivation myth

Traditional approaches to motivation assume that people can generate sustained effort for important goals through cognitive commitment and planning. This works for neurotypical brains but often fails for ADHD brains that require different neurochemical conditions for sustained engagement.

"Should" motivation doesn't work: ADHD brains don't respond well to motivation based on "should," "have to," or "need to." These external imperatives don't generate enough dopamine to sustain attention and effort over time.

Delayed gratification challenges: Goals with distant payoffs struggle to compete with immediate, stimulating alternatives. An ADHD brain might fully understand that completing a work project is important but still gravitate toward more immediately rewarding activities.

Inconsistent motivation: Motivation levels can vary dramatically based on energy, interest, novelty, and external stimulation. Someone with ADHD might be highly motivated on Monday and completely unmotivated on Tuesday for the same exact goal.

Interest-based neurochemistry

ADHD brains function optimally when engaged with personally interesting, novel, or challenging material. This isn't preference or personality—it's neurochemistry. Interesting activities trigger dopamine release that supports attention, working memory, and executive function.

Hyperfocus as strength: The same attention regulation differences that cause distractibility also enable intense focus when the right conditions are present. Many people with ADHD can sustain attention for hours on personally interesting projects.

Novelty seeking: ADHD brains are naturally drawn to new, different, or changing stimuli because novelty triggers dopamine release. This can look like distractibility but it's actually the brain seeking optimal functioning conditions.

Challenge engagement: Tasks that are appropriately challenging (not too easy, not too hard) can maintain ADHD attention through the dopamine release that comes from problem-solving and skill building.

Interest-based vs. importance-based tasks

One of the most crucial distinctions in ADHD-adapted motivational interviewing is understanding the difference between tasks that capture interest and tasks that feel important. Traditional MI assumes these categories overlap significantly, but for ADHD brains, they often don't align at all.

The interest-importance gap

Many ADHD individuals experience a painful gap between what interests their brain and what they intellectually know is important. This creates internal conflict and shame that traditional therapeutic approaches often misunderstand.

High interest, low importance: Activities that capture natural ADHD attention (social media, games, learning about fascinating topics, creative projects) often feel less "productive" or important to external standards.

High importance, low interest: Essential life tasks (paying bills, completing paperwork, routine maintenance, boring work projects) often provide insufficient stimulation to maintain ADHD attention despite clear importance.

The productivity guilt cycle: ADHD individuals often feel guilty about spending time on interesting activities and frustrated about struggling with important ones, creating a shame cycle that interferes with effective goal-setting.

Maria, a 34-year-old with ADHD, explains her daily struggle: "I can spend three hours researching the perfect vacation I can't afford, but I can't make myself spend twenty minutes paying bills. I know the bills are more important, but my brain just won't engage with them. Then I feel guilty about the vacation research and stressed about the unpaid bills, and the whole thing becomes this horrible cycle."

Working with interest patterns

Instead of fighting against ADHD interest patterns, effective MI approaches leverage them strategically.

Interest archaeology: Help people identify what types of activities, topics, and formats naturally capture their attention. What can they focus on for hours without effort? What kinds of problems do they solve effortlessly? What topics do they research spontaneously?

Pattern recognition: Look for commonalities across high-interest activities. Do they involve problem-solving? Creativity? Social interaction? Learning? Competition? Movement? Understanding these patterns helps identify ways to make important tasks more engaging.

Interest bridging: Find connections between natural interests and important goals. Someone fascinated by psychology might approach relationship goals through understanding social dynamics. Someone interested in technology might track personal goals through apps and data analysis.

Reimagining importance through interest

Rather than trying to make ADHD brains care about inherently boring tasks, find ways to connect important goals to inherently interesting elements.

Gamification strategies: Transform routine tasks into games, competitions, or challenges that provide more immediate feedback and stimulation.

Social accountability: Many ADHD individuals find social elements (accountability partners, body doubling, group challenges) add interest and energy to otherwise boring tasks.

Learning integration: Frame important tasks as learning opportunities, research projects, or skill-building exercises that satisfy the ADHD brain's craving for novelty and growth.

Creative approaches: Find unconventional, creative, or personalized ways to accomplish necessary goals that align with individual interests and thinking patterns.

The productivity reframe

Help ADHD individuals develop a broader definition of productivity that includes interest-based activities and recognizes their value.

Creative productivity: Time spent on creative projects, learning, or exploring interests isn't wasted—it's often when ADHD brains produce their best work and generate insights that benefit other life areas.

Restoration value: Engaging with high-interest activities provides neurochemical restoration that makes it possible to tackle lower-interest necessary tasks.

Skill transfer: Abilities developed through interest-based activities (research skills, creative problem-solving, technical expertise) often transfer to other life domains in unexpected ways.

Energy management: Rather than viewing interest-based activities as procrastination, recognize them as energy sources that fuel overall functioning.

Creating immediate rewards and feedback

ADHD brains struggle with delayed gratification not because of character flaws but because of neurochemical realities. Effective MI approaches work with this reality by building immediate rewards and feedback into change processes.

The immediacy principle

Traditional goal-setting often focuses on distant outcomes (lose 20 pounds, complete degree, save $5000) that don't provide enough immediate reinforcement to sustain ADHD motivation. Successful approaches break goals into components that provide frequent, immediate rewards.

Micro-goals with instant feedback: Instead of "exercise more," create daily movement goals with immediate tracking. Instead of "organize house," focus on single rooms or even single drawers with immediate visual satisfaction.

Process rewards vs. outcome rewards: ADHD brains often respond better to rewards for effort and process rather than just outcomes. Reward yourself for showing up, trying, or following through, not just for perfect results.

Celebration integration: Build celebration and acknowledgment into the change process rather than waiting until major milestones are reached.

Immediate feedback systems

Create systems that provide quick, clear information about progress and effort.

Visual progress tracking: Charts, apps, calendars, or other visual systems that show daily or weekly progress provide immediate feedback that sustains motivation.

Body doubling and accountability: Having someone witness efforts and provide immediate encouragement or acknowledgment satisfies the ADHD need for external validation and feedback.

Technology integration: Apps, timers, notifications, and other technological tools can provide immediate feedback and gamification elements that sustain engagement.

Environmental feedback: Arrange environments so that progress is immediately visible—clean spaces stay visible, completed tasks leave obvious evidence, improvements are apparent.

Reward scheduling strategies

Build reward systems that honor ADHD neurochemistry rather than fighting against it.

High-frequency small rewards: Many small, frequent rewards work better than infrequent large rewards for maintaining ADHD motivation over time.

Interest-based rewards: Use activities that naturally generate dopamine (creative time, social interaction, learning opportunities) as rewards for completing lower-interest necessary tasks.

Variety and novelty: Rotate rewards to maintain novelty and prevent habituation. What works as motivation this week might lose effectiveness next week.

Social rewards: Many ADHD individuals are highly motivated by social connection, recognition, or the opportunity to help others.

David discovered that he could maintain his exercise routine by pairing it with podcasts about topics he found fascinating. The intellectual stimulation combined with physical movement provided enough dopamine to sustain the habit. He also scheduled exercise immediately before activities he naturally enjoyed, creating a reward sequence that worked with his brain's motivation patterns.

Sustaining motivation through conversation

Traditional MI conversations assume that people can maintain focus and engagement throughout 45-50 minute sessions focused on change planning and goal exploration. ADHD brains often need different conversational approaches to sustain engagement and benefit from therapeutic discussions.

Conversational pace and variety

ADHD brains often think quickly and crave stimulation, requiring conversational approaches that match their cognitive pace and interest needs.

Faster pace accommodation: Allow for quicker topic exploration, rapid idea generation, and faster conversational flow rather than insisting on slow, thorough processing of single topics.

Topic variety integration: Include multiple related topics in single sessions rather than exhaustive exploration of single issues. ADHD brains often benefit from seeing connections between different life areas.

Interactive elements: Incorporate movement, visual tools, hands-on activities, or other interactive elements that provide stimulation and support attention.

Energy matching: Pay attention to the person's energy levels and adjust conversational intensity accordingly. High-energy times might support rapid problem-solving while lower-energy times might be better for reflection or planning.

Attention and engagement maintenance

Structure conversations to work with ADHD attention patterns rather than against them.

Interest hooks: Begin sessions with topics or questions that naturally capture attention before moving to more challenging or boring material.

Movement integration: Allow and encourage fidgeting, walking, or other movement that supports attention and engagement rather than viewing it as distraction.

Stimulation balancing: Some ADHD individuals need more environmental stimulation (background music, visual aids) while others need less. Adjust the environment to support individual attention needs.

Break integration: Build in natural breaks, topic shifts, or activity changes to prevent attention fatigue and maintain engagement throughout longer sessions.

Working with ADHD time perception

Time blindness—difficulty accurately perceiving time passage—significantly affects how ADHD individuals experience goal-setting and progress tracking.

External time supports: Use timers, clocks, calendars, and other external tools to provide time awareness during goal-setting and planning discussions.

Time estimation practice: Help people develop more accurate time estimation skills through practice and feedback rather than assuming they can mentally track time requirements for tasks.

Buffer time integration: Build extra time into all plans and schedules to accommodate the reality that ADHD individuals often underestimate time requirements.

Time-flexible planning: Create plans that can accommodate variations in energy, attention, and time availability rather than rigid schedules that set people up for failure.

Motivation momentum strategies

Help people understand and work with their natural motivation patterns rather than expecting consistent motivation levels.

Energy awareness: Help people identify their natural energy and motivation patterns throughout days and weeks so they can schedule important activities during optimal times.

Momentum capitalization: When motivation is high, use that energy for planning, preparation, or tackling multiple related tasks rather than limiting focus to single goals.

Low-motivation planning: Develop strategies for low-motivation periods that maintain progress without requiring high energy or engagement.

Transition support: Create specific strategies for reengaging with goals after periods of low motivation or life disruption.

Jennifer learned to identify her natural motivation patterns and schedule accordingly. She discovered she had high energy and focus in the mornings and after workouts, so she scheduled important tasks during these times. For low-energy periods, she created simple, minimal-effort maintenance routines that kept her goals moving forward without requiring high motivation. Her therapist helped her see this as working with her brain rather than being inconsistent or unreliable.

The key insight is that ADHD brains aren't broken or lacking willpower—they're neurochemically different and require different approaches to motivation and change. When we work with dopamine-driven patterns rather than against them, ADHD individuals often demonstrate remarkable creativity, intensity, and capability in pursuing their goals.

The next chapter explores how executive function differences in ADHD require specific adaptations to the planning and organization aspects of motivational interviewing, moving from general motivation to practical implementation support.

Harnessing the ADHD advantage

ADHD motivation operates on fundamentally different neurochemical principles than neurotypical motivation systems. Rather than viewing this as a deficit to overcome, effective MI approaches leverage the unique strengths of dopamine-driven brains: intense focus on interesting material, creative problem-solving, rapid thinking, and high energy when properly engaged.

The breakthrough comes from aligning therapeutic goals with ADHD neurochemistry rather than fighting against it. This means prioritizing interest over importance, building immediate rewards into change processes, and creating conversational approaches that match ADHD pace and stimulation needs.

This approach often reveals remarkable capabilities and enthusiasm that remain hidden when ADHD individuals try to force themselves into neurotypical motivation patterns.

Chapter 9: Executive Function Support

Planning and organization MI

When Lisa's therapist asked her what specific steps she would take to achieve her goal of "getting more organized," Lisa's response revealed the hidden challenge of ADHD executive functioning: "I know I need to get organized. I can see exactly how organized I want my apartment to look. I've watched YouTube videos about organization systems. I've bought containers and labels. But somehow, I can never figure out the actual steps to get from where I am now to where I want to be. It's like there's this massive gap between knowing what I want and knowing how to make it happen."

Lisa wasn't lacking motivation or commitment—she was experiencing executive function challenges that make the planning and sequencing aspects of change particularly difficult for ADHD brains. Traditional motivational interviewing assumes that people can naturally break down goals into actionable steps, estimate time requirements accurately, and follow through on plans consistently. For individuals with ADHD, these assumptions often don't hold.

Dr. Martinez, Lisa's therapist, realized that effective MI with ADHD individuals requires providing explicit executive function support rather than expecting people to manage complex planning tasks independently.

Breaking down complex changes into manageable steps

Executive function encompasses the brain's management system—the abilities to plan, organize, prioritize, estimate time, and coordinate multiple tasks toward goal achievement. ADHD significantly affects these capacities, making complex changes feel overwhelming even when motivation is high.

The executive function bottleneck

Many ADHD individuals experience a bottleneck between wanting to change and being able to execute change plans. They often have clear vision for their goals and strong motivation but struggle with the organizational and planning skills required for implementation.

Planning paralysis: Complex goals can feel so overwhelming that people don't know where to start, leading to procrastination or avoidance despite genuine desire for change.

Step blindness: The ability to see the logical sequence of steps between current state and desired outcome doesn't come naturally to many ADHD brains.

Detail overwhelm: When ADHD individuals do attempt planning, they might get lost in excessive details or fail to identify which details are actually important.

Priority confusion: Everything feels equally important or urgent, making it difficult to determine what to focus on first.

The collaborative planning approach

Rather than expecting ADHD individuals to generate plans independently, provide collaborative support for breaking down complex changes into manageable components.

External planning support: Serve as an external executive function system by helping organize thoughts, sequence steps, and maintain focus during planning discussions.

Concrete step identification: Help translate abstract goals into specific, observable actions. "Get organized" becomes "sort clothes into keep/donate piles," then "put keep clothes back in closet using new system."

Logical sequencing: Work together to identify the logical order of steps, paying attention to dependencies (what needs to happen before what) and resource requirements.

Size calibration: Help people accurately estimate the scope and complexity of different steps to avoid overwhelming themselves with unrealistic expectations.

The backwards planning method

Start with the end goal and work backwards to identify necessary steps, which often feels more manageable for ADHD brains than forward planning.

"Let's start with your vision of having an organized apartment. What would that look like specifically? Now, what would need to be true the day before you reached that goal? What about the week before? Let's work backwards to figure out the path."

This approach leverages the ADHD ability to visualize desired outcomes while providing structure for the sequential thinking that often presents challenges.

Micro-step development

Break goals into steps that are small enough to feel achievable even during low-motivation periods.

The 10-minute rule: Each step should be accomplishable in 10-15 minutes or less to prevent overwhelm and enable progress during brief motivation windows.

Single-focus tasks: Each step should involve only one type of activity to reduce cognitive switching costs and simplify execution.

Clear completion criteria: Define exactly what "done" looks like for each step to prevent perfectionism from blocking progress.

Energy matching: Identify which steps require high energy and which can be done during low-energy periods, creating options for different mental states.

Marcus wanted to apply to graduate school but felt paralyzed by the complexity of the application process. His therapist helped him break the process into micro-steps: "Research five programs" became "spend 15 minutes looking at websites for Program A," then "write three sentences about Program A requirements," then "find contact information for Program A admissions office." Each step was small enough to complete in a single focused session, reducing overwhelm and building momentum.

Supporting planning and follow-through

ADHD individuals often excel at generating ideas and initial planning but struggle with consistent follow-through on established plans. Effective MI approaches provide ongoing support for plan implementation rather than assuming that good initial planning will lead to automatic execution.

The implementation gap

There's often a significant gap between making plans and executing them consistently for ADHD individuals. This gap isn't about commitment or desire—it's about the ongoing executive function demands of plan execution.

Working memory challenges: People might forget elements of their plans, lose track of where they are in multi-step processes, or become confused about what comes next.

Flexibility paralysis: When original plans don't work out perfectly, ADHD individuals might abandon them entirely rather than adapting flexibly to new circumstances.

Momentum maintenance: Starting tasks is often easier than sustaining effort through completion, leading to many partially completed projects.

Context switching difficulties: Moving between different types of tasks or returning to interrupted projects can be cognitively demanding.

External executive function tools

Provide external systems that support the executive function demands of plan implementation.

Written action plans: Create detailed written plans that serve as external memory and can be referenced when working memory fails.

Progress tracking systems: Develop visual or digital systems for tracking progress through multi-step plans, providing both accountability and satisfaction.

Reminder systems: Build reminder systems (alarms, calendar notifications, accountability partners) that prompt plan execution without relying on internal memory.

Environmental supports: Arrange physical environments to support plan execution by reducing barriers and providing visual cues.

The accountability partnership model

Many ADHD individuals benefit from external accountability that provides structure without judgment.

Regular check-ins: Schedule frequent, brief check-ins about plan progress rather than infrequent, lengthy review sessions.

Problem-solving support: When plans aren't working, collaborate on modifications rather than abandoning goals or maintaining ineffective approaches.

Celebration integration: Acknowledge progress and effort regularly rather than waiting for complete goal achievement.

Obstacle anticipation: Proactively identify potential barriers to plan execution and develop strategies for addressing them before they derail progress.

Flexible plan adaptation

Help people develop skills for adapting plans when circumstances change rather than viewing plan modifications as failures.

Plan B development: For important goals, develop alternative approaches that can be used when primary plans don't work out.

Progress preservation: When plans need modification, identify what progress has been made and how to build on it rather than starting over completely.

Circumstance responsiveness: Teach people to adjust plans based on energy levels, time availability, and changing life circumstances rather than rigidly adhering to original timelines.

Learning integration: Frame plan modifications as learning opportunities that provide information for developing more effective future plans.

Working with time blindness and poor estimation

Time blindness—difficulty accurately perceiving time passage and estimating time requirements—significantly affects planning and goal achievement for ADHD individuals. Traditional MI approaches often underestimate how profoundly time perception differences impact change processes.

Understanding ADHD time perception

ADHD brains often experience time differently than neurotypical brains, affecting both moment-to-moment time awareness and long-term planning abilities.

Time passage awareness: Many ADHD individuals have difficulty sensing how much time has passed during activities, leading to underestimating task duration or losing track of schedules.

Future time estimation: Accurately predicting how long tasks will take requires executive function skills that are often impaired in ADHD, leading to chronically overpacked schedules and unrealistic expectations.

Time horizon variations: ADHD individuals might be very focused on immediate timeframes but struggle with longer-term temporal planning, or vice versa.

Interest-dependent time perception: Time perception can vary dramatically based on task interest—hours might feel like minutes during engaging activities but minutes feel like hours during boring ones.

Time estimation support strategies

Provide external support for developing more accurate time estimation and time management skills.

Time tracking exercises: Help people track actual time requirements for routine activities to develop more accurate internal estimates.

Buffer time integration: Build additional time into all plans to accommodate the reality of time underestimation without creating frustration or self-criticism.

Timer utilization: Encourage use of external timers for both time awareness during tasks and time estimation practice.

Time categorization: Help people develop categories for different types of time requirements (5-minute tasks, 30-minute tasks, half-day projects) to improve estimation accuracy.

Schedule realism development

Help people create realistic schedules that account for ADHD-specific time challenges.

Energy-based scheduling: Plan demanding tasks during high-energy periods and lighter tasks during predictable low-energy times.

Transition time inclusion: Build time for transitions between tasks, especially when they involve different types of thinking or physical locations.

Flexibility buffers: Include unscheduled time in daily and weekly plans to accommodate unexpected delays, energy fluctuations, or opportunity for hyperfocus sessions.

Recovery time planning: Schedule downtime after demanding activities to prevent overscheduling and burnout.

Sarah learned to work with her time blindness by building 50% buffer time into all her estimates. If she thought a task would take one hour, she scheduled 90 minutes. Initially, this felt like admitting failure, but her therapist helped her reframe it as working skillfully with her brain's reality rather than fighting against it. Over time, Sarah's follow-through improved dramatically because her plans became achievable rather than aspirational.

Visual and external organization tools

ADHD brains often benefit from external organizational systems that provide structure, visual cues, and memory support. Rather than expecting people to develop internal organizational skills, effective approaches leverage external tools that work with ADHD cognitive patterns.

Visual organization principles

Many ADHD individuals are visual processors who benefit from organizational systems that provide immediate visual information about tasks, progress, and priorities.

Visual task management: Use charts, calendars, kanban boards, or other visual systems that show task status at a glance rather than relying on mental tracking.

Color coding systems: Organize information by color to reduce cognitive load and support quick categorization and retrieval.

Physical visibility: Keep important items, reminders, and tools visually accessible rather than stored away where they might be forgotten.

Progress visualization: Create systems that make progress visible and satisfying, such as charts that can be checked off or visual representations of goal achievement.

Digital tool integration

Leverage technology to provide external executive function support that works with ADHD cognitive patterns.

App-based organization: Use smartphone apps for task management, reminders, time tracking, and progress monitoring that provide immediate access and feedback.

Automated systems: Set up automated reminders, bill payments, and other routine systems that reduce the ongoing executive function load of daily life management.

Synchronization across devices: Ensure organizational tools are accessible across all devices and locations to prevent information silos and missed tasks.

Notification management: Use push notifications and alerts strategically to provide timely reminders without creating overwhelm or distraction.

Environmental design for executive function

Arrange physical environments to support planning, organization, and follow-through rather than requiring people to overcome environmental obstacles.

Task-specific spaces: Create designated areas for different types of activities (planning space, creative space, administrative tasks) that provide appropriate tools and minimize distractions.

Visual cue placement: Position reminders, calendars, and organizational tools in highly visible locations where they'll be noticed regularly.

Barrier reduction: Remove obstacles that make desirable behaviors more difficult and add obstacles that make undesirable behaviors less automatic.

Reset systems: Create simple systems for returning spaces to organized states after use, making maintenance easier than reorganization.

Paper-based backup systems

Despite digital advantages, many ADHD individuals benefit from physical, tangible organizational tools that provide different types of cognitive support.

Physical calendars and planners: Large, visible calendars that show monthly or weekly overviews can provide spatial and temporal awareness that digital calendars sometimes lack.

Notebook systems: Capture thoughts, plans, and information in physical notebooks that can be carried and accessed without digital distractions.

Post-it note strategies: Use physical sticky notes for immediate reminders and visual cues that are harder to ignore than digital notifications.

Wall charts and displays: Create large visual displays of goals, progress, or important information that provide constant visual reinforcement.

Tom developed a hybrid system combining digital and physical tools. He used a smartphone app for detailed task management and reminders but maintained a large wall calendar showing monthly goals and a physical notebook for daily planning and reflection. The combination provided both the convenience of digital tools and the visual/tactile benefits of physical systems. His therapist helped him recognize that using multiple systems wasn't inefficient—it was working with his brain's need for varied input and external support.

The key insight is that executive function challenges in ADHD aren't character flaws or laziness—they're neurological differences that require external support systems and adapted approaches. When we provide appropriate scaffolding for planning, organization, and follow-through, ADHD individuals often demonstrate remarkable goal achievement abilities that remained hidden when they tried to rely solely on internal executive function skills.

The next chapter addresses the movement and energy aspects of ADHD that significantly affect therapeutic engagement and change processes, exploring how to channel rather than suppress hyperactivity and impulsivity.

Supporting the ADHD executive system

Executive function challenges in ADHD create a gap between motivation and implementation that traditional MI approaches often fail to address. The solution isn't trying to develop better internal executive skills but providing external systems and collaborative support that work with ADHD cognitive patterns.

Successful approaches break complex changes into micro-steps, provide ongoing implementation support, account for time perception differences, and leverage visual and technological tools to reduce cognitive load. This transforms executive function challenges from barriers into manageable aspects of the change process.

When ADHD individuals receive appropriate executive function support, they often demonstrate impressive goal achievement capabilities that surprise both themselves and others who have observed their previous struggles with follow-through.

Chapter 10: Hyperactivity and Impulsivity

Channel versus change

Dr. Thompson was twenty minutes into her session with 16-year-old Alex when she noticed his knee bouncing rapidly under the table, his pen clicking in a steady rhythm, and his eyes darting frequently to the window. Her traditional MI training suggested that these behaviors indicated distraction or disengagement, so she gently asked him to "try to focus" and put the pen down.

What Dr. Thompson didn't understand was that Alex's movement wasn't interfering with his attention—it was supporting it. The bouncing knee, pen clicking, and visual scanning weren't signs of poor focus but rather his brain's attempts to generate the stimulation needed for optimal cognitive functioning.

When Alex stopped moving, his ability to process their conversation actually decreased. His responses became shorter, less detailed, and he seemed to "check out" mentally. Dr. Thompson was inadvertently working against Alex's neurological needs rather than with them.

The breakthrough came when she learned to view hyperactivity and impulsivity as features of Alex's brain that could be channeled productively rather than problems to eliminate.

Incorporating movement into MI conversations

For many individuals with ADHD, movement isn't a distraction from thinking—it's a requirement for optimal cognitive functioning. Traditional therapeutic settings often inadvertently impair ADHD functioning by expecting stillness and sustained sitting that goes against neurological needs for movement and stimulation.

Understanding movement as cognitive support

Hyperactivity in ADHD serves important neurological functions that support rather than interfere with attention and learning.

Arousal regulation: Movement helps regulate arousal levels in the brain, bringing ADHD individuals to optimal states for attention and cognitive processing.

Dopamine generation: Physical movement stimulates dopamine production, which ADHD brains need for sustained attention and executive functioning.

Sensory integration: Many ADHD individuals have sensory processing differences that make movement necessary for feeling comfortable and regulated in their bodies.

Working memory support: Research suggests that appropriate movement can actually improve working memory and cognitive performance in ADHD individuals (Sarver et al., 2015).

Fidgeting as focus: What appears to be distraction often represents the brain's attempt to create optimal conditions for attention and engagement.

Movement-friendly therapeutic environments

Create therapeutic spaces that support rather than suppress natural movement needs.

Flexible seating options: Provide choices beyond traditional chairs—exercise balls, rocking chairs, standing desks, or floor cushions that allow for movement variation.

Fidget tools availability: Keep stress balls, fidget cubes, textured objects, or other tactile tools available for those who benefit from hand movement during conversation.

Movement breaks integration: Build regular movement breaks into longer sessions rather than expecting sustained stillness throughout entire appointments.

Walking meetings: Consider conducting some therapeutic conversations while walking, which can enhance both engagement and creative problem-solving for many ADHD individuals.

Space for pacing: Arrange furniture to allow for natural pacing or position changes during conversations without creating disruption.

Movement-integrated MI techniques

Adapt traditional MI techniques to incorporate movement in ways that enhance rather than distract from therapeutic work.

Standing scaling exercises: When using scaling questions, have people physically position themselves in space to represent their confidence or motivation levels rather than just verbally reporting numbers.

Walking reflection: Conduct some reflective conversations during walks, allowing for the gentle stimulation of movement while processing important topics.

Active goal-setting: Use physical props, drawing, or movement-based activities to explore goals and develop plans rather than relying solely on verbal discussion.

Kinesthetic metaphors: Use physical analogies and movement-based metaphors that align with ADHD preferences for concrete, experiential learning.

Energy matching: Adjust the energy level of conversations to match the person's current arousal state rather than insisting on consistent low-energy processing.

Jessica, a 25-year-old with ADHD, struggled with traditional therapy because sitting still made her feel anxious and restless. Her therapist adapted by providing a variety of fidget tools and suggesting they conduct some sessions while walking around the building. Jessica discovered that she could access deeper insights and more creative solutions when her body was gently active during conversations. The movement helped her brain reach optimal functioning levels for therapeutic work.

Managing impulsive responses and decisions

Impulsivity in ADHD involves both challenges and strengths that require nuanced approaches in therapeutic settings. Rather than simply trying to reduce impulsive responses, effective MI approaches help people channel impulsive energy productively while developing skills for situations where impulse control is necessary.

Understanding ADHD impulsivity

Impulsivity in ADHD stems from neurological differences in inhibitory control and delayed gratification rather than character flaws or poor decision-making abilities.

Executive function delays: The brain regions responsible for "thinking before acting" often develop more slowly and function differently in ADHD, making immediate response inhibition challenging.

Emotional intensity: ADHD individuals often experience emotions more intensely and have difficulty modulating emotional responses, leading to impulsive reactions during emotionally charged situations.

Interest-driven decisions: Impulsive choices often align with immediate interests or excitement rather than long-term planning considerations.

Hyperfocus transitions: Moving from intense focus on one activity to another can create transition challenges that look like impulsive behavior.

Channeling impulsive energy productively

Rather than viewing impulsivity as purely problematic, help people identify ways to channel impulsive tendencies toward positive outcomes.

Rapid decision-making strengths: Many ADHD individuals excel at quick decision-making in dynamic situations and can be valuable contributors in fast-paced environments.

Creative spontaneity: Impulsive responses often lead to creative solutions, innovative approaches, and original thinking that more cautious individuals might miss.

Enthusiasm and energy: The same impulsivity that creates challenges can also fuel passion projects, spontaneous learning, and energetic engagement with interesting goals.

Social spontaneity: ADHD impulsivity can contribute to social warmth, humor, and authentic connection in interpersonal relationships.

Developing pause strategies

Help people develop skills for creating brief pauses when impulse control is important without eliminating spontaneity entirely.

The ADHD pause: Develop personalized strategies for creating brief moments between impulse and action—counting to three, taking a deep breath, or asking a standard question like "Is this urgent or just interesting?"

Environmental supports: Arrange environments to provide natural pauses (removing triggers, adding steps to impulsive behaviors) while maintaining access to positive impulsive opportunities.

Energy redirection: When impulsive energy arises, practice channeling it toward productive activities rather than simply suppressing it.

Context awareness: Help people identify situations where impulsivity is more or less problematic, developing different strategies for different contexts.

Working with emotional impulsivity

ADHD individuals often experience intense emotional reactions that can lead to impulsive responses in therapeutic settings and daily life.

Emotional intensity normalization: Help people understand that intense emotional responses are part of ADHD neurology rather than character flaws or overreactions.

Regulation skills development: Build specific skills for managing emotional intensity, including sensory strategies, movement options, and cognitive techniques.

Communication adaptations: Develop ways to express intense emotions effectively without creating interpersonal problems or therapeutic disruption.

Recovery strategies: Create approaches for addressing impulsive emotional responses after they occur, including repair strategies and learning opportunities.

Fidgeting as focus tool, not distraction

One of the most important shifts in ADHD-informed therapeutic practice is reconceptualizing fidgeting and restless movement as cognitive support rather than problematic behavior. This reframe changes everything about how therapeutic relationships develop and how effective interventions become.

The neuroscience of fidgeting

Research increasingly supports the idea that fidgeting and small movements actually enhance cognitive performance for many ADHD individuals rather than interfering with it.

Attention regulation: Fidgeting helps regulate attention by providing just enough stimulation to keep the ADHD brain in optimal arousal zones for learning and processing.

Working memory enhancement: Some studies suggest that appropriate movement and fidgeting can improve working memory performance in ADHD individuals (Hartanto et al., 2016).

Sensory satisfaction: Fidgeting often provides sensory input that helps ADHD individuals feel more comfortable and regulated in their bodies.

Cognitive rhythm: Many people have natural rhythms of movement that support their thinking patterns and cognitive processing.

Fidget-friendly therapeutic practices

Create therapeutic environments that support rather than suppress natural fidgeting and movement needs.

Tool availability: Keep various fidget tools readily available—stress balls, thinking putty, textured strips on table edges, or small handheld objects that provide tactile stimulation.

Movement permission: Explicitly communicate that movement and fidgeting are welcome and helpful rather than problematic or distracting.

Individual preferences: Learn what types of movement and stimulation work best for each individual—some prefer hand movements, others benefit from foot movement, and some need larger body movements.

Discrete options: Provide fidgeting options that don't interfere with conversation or become distracting to others while still meeting sensory needs.

Distinguishing supportive from disruptive movement

Help people identify which types of movement enhance their functioning versus which might actually interfere with attention or social interaction.

Attention-supporting movement: Generally rhythmic, repetitive, or consistent movements that provide steady stimulation without requiring cognitive attention.

Potentially disruptive movement: Activities that require significant cognitive attention, create social distraction, or interfere with task completion.

Context-appropriate adaptations: Develop skills for adapting movement needs to different situations—what works in therapy might need modification for work meetings or academic settings.

Self-advocacy development: Build skills for communicating movement needs to others and advocating for accommodations in various settings.

The focus paradox

Help ADHD individuals understand the counterintuitive relationship between movement and attention that often confuses both them and others around them.

Stillness impairment: For many ADHD brains, forced stillness actually decreases cognitive capacity and attention rather than improving it.

Movement optimization: There's often an optimal level of movement that maximizes cognitive functioning—too little and attention wanes, too much and it becomes genuinely distracting.

Individual variation: Movement needs vary significantly between individuals and can change based on energy levels, task demands, and environmental factors.

Social misunderstanding: Help people navigate social situations where their movement needs might be misinterpreted by others who don't understand ADHD neurology.

Energy channeling strategies

ADHD individuals often have high levels of mental and physical energy that can be either productive resources or sources of difficulty depending on how they're managed and channeled. Effective approaches work with this energy rather than trying to suppress or ignore it.

Understanding ADHD energy patterns

Energy levels and patterns in ADHD often differ significantly from neurotypical patterns and require different management approaches.

Variable energy cycles: Energy levels can fluctuate dramatically throughout days and weeks, requiring flexible approaches that work with these natural rhythms.

Intensity variations: ADHD individuals might experience periods of extremely high energy followed by exhaustion or low-energy periods.

Interest-driven energy: Energy levels often correspond closely to interest levels—fascinating topics or activities can generate sustained high energy while boring tasks deplete energy rapidly.

Physical-mental connection: Physical energy and mental energy are often closely connected in ADHD, with movement supporting cognitive functioning and sedentary periods potentially decreasing mental clarity.

Productive energy channeling

Help people identify ways to channel high energy periods into productive activities that align with their goals and values.

Energy-activity matching: Identify which activities work best during high-energy periods versus which are appropriate for lower-energy times.

Hyperfocus leveraging: Use high-energy periods for tasks that can benefit from intense focus and sustained attention.

Creative project timing: Schedule creative, brainstorming, or innovative work during natural high-energy periods when ADHD strengths are most accessible.

Physical activity integration: Use physical exercise or movement activities to channel excess physical energy in ways that support rather than compete with other goals.

Energy regulation techniques

Develop skills for managing energy levels to maintain sustainable functioning over time.

Energy awareness: Help people identify their personal energy patterns and learn to recognize early signs of energy shifts.

Regulation strategies: Build toolkit of techniques for increasing energy when needed and channeling or calming excessive energy when appropriate.

Recovery planning: Develop approaches for recovering from high-energy periods without experiencing complete burnout or depletion.

Environmental energy management: Identify environmental factors that support or drain energy and make adjustments when possible.

Mike discovered that his ADHD energy patterns were his greatest asset when properly managed. He learned to schedule his most challenging work projects during his natural high-energy periods (usually late morning and mid-afternoon) while using lower-energy times for routine tasks and administration. He built regular exercise into his schedule to channel physical energy productively and developed strategies for recognizing when he was pushing too hard and needed rest. His therapist helped him reframe his variable energy as a resource to work with rather than a problem to solve.

The fundamental shift is moving from trying to make ADHD individuals sit still and behave like neurotypical people to creating environments and approaches that leverage their natural energy, movement needs, and impulsive strengths while building skills for situations that require different approaches.

The next chapter addresses one of the most challenging aspects of ADHD that significantly impacts therapeutic relationships and change motivation: rejection sensitive dysphoria and its effects on how individuals respond to feedback, setbacks, and interpersonal interactions.

Working with ADHD energy

Hyperactivity and impulsivity in ADHD represent neurological differences that can be channeled productively rather than problems to eliminate. Movement supports cognitive functioning for many ADHD brains, and impulsive energy can fuel creativity, enthusiasm, and rapid decision-making when appropriately directed.

The key insight is that successful therapeutic approaches work with ADHD energy patterns rather than against them. This means creating movement-friendly environments, channeling impulsive energy toward productive goals, supporting fidgeting as a focus tool, and helping people optimize their natural energy cycles for maximum effectiveness.

This reframe often transforms ADHD traits from sources of shame and frustration into recognized strengths and resources for achieving personal goals.

Chapter 11: RSD and Motivation

Rejection sensitive dysphoria considerations

The session started normally enough. Dr. Rivera was working with 28-year-old Hannah on developing better work-life balance. When Dr. Rivera gently suggested that Hannah might benefit from setting clearer boundaries with her supervisor, Hannah's entire demeanor shifted instantly. Her shoulders hunched, her voice became small and defensive, and she said, "So you think I'm weak and can't handle my job. You think I'm just complaining and making excuses."

Dr. Rivera was confused by the intensity of Hannah's reaction to what she'd intended as supportive feedback. She didn't realize that Hannah was experiencing rejection sensitive dysphoria (RSD)—a common but poorly understood aspect of ADHD that causes extreme emotional sensitivity to perceived criticism, disapproval, or rejection.

What felt like gentle guidance to Dr. Rivera registered as harsh judgment to Hannah's ADHD brain. **The very therapeutic techniques designed to support change felt threatening and shameful to someone experiencing RSD.** This misunderstanding derailed their therapeutic relationship and made Hannah less likely to engage honestly in future sessions.

Dr. Rivera learned that working effectively with ADHD individuals requires understanding how RSD affects their responses to feedback, setbacks, and interpersonal interactions in therapeutic contexts.

Understanding emotional dysregulation in ADHD

Rejection Sensitive Dysphoria is a neurological feature of ADHD that involves intense emotional reactions to real or perceived rejection, criticism, or disapproval. While not yet included in official diagnostic criteria, RSD affects an estimated 99% of individuals with ADHD and significantly impacts their relationships, self-concept, and willingness to take risks or pursue goals (Dodson, 2020).

The neurobiological basis of RSD

RSD isn't a character flaw, emotional immaturity, or learned behavior—it's a neurobiological feature of ADHD that affects how the brain processes social and emotional information.

Emotional dysregulation in ADHD: The same executive function differences that affect attention and impulse control also impact emotional regulation, making emotional responses more intense and harder to modulate.

Social threat sensitivity: ADHD brains often have heightened sensitivity to social threats, interpreting neutral or mildly negative social cues as significantly more threatening than neurotypical brains would.

Rejection detection systems: The neurological systems responsible for detecting social rejection appear to be hyperactive in many ADHD individuals, leading to false alarms and overreactions to perceived social threats.

Emotional recovery delays: While neurotypical individuals might recover from criticism or rejection relatively quickly, ADHD individuals often experience prolonged emotional impacts that can last days or weeks.

Common RSD triggers in therapeutic settings

Traditional MI techniques can inadvertently trigger RSD responses if not carefully adapted for emotional sensitivity.

Gentle confrontation: Even supportive challenges to thinking patterns or behaviors can feel like harsh criticism to someone with RSD.

Reflective feedback: Having behaviors or emotions reflected back can feel like judgment or disapproval rather than supportive mirroring.

Goal-setting discussions: Talking about areas for change can trigger shame about current inadequacies rather than hope about future possibilities.

Progress reviews: Discussing areas where progress has been limited can feel like failure feedback rather than problem-solving opportunities.

Therapeutic silence: Pauses in conversation might be interpreted as disapproval, boredom, or judgment rather than reflective space.

The perfectionism connection

RSD often drives perfectionist tendencies as individuals attempt to avoid any possibility of criticism or rejection.

All-or-nothing thinking: Fear of partial success being perceived as failure can lead to avoiding goals entirely or setting unrealistic standards.

Procrastination patterns: Rather than risk imperfect performance, individuals might delay starting important tasks indefinitely.

Achievement pressure: Constant worry about meeting others' expectations can create unsustainable pressure and burnout.

Social masking: Many ADHD individuals develop elaborate strategies for hiding their struggles to avoid perceived judgment, which is exhausting and unsustainable.

Creating psychologically safe conversation spaces

Effective MI with RSD-sensitive individuals requires creating therapeutic environments that minimize RSD triggers while maintaining the supportive challenge necessary for growth and change.

RSD-informed therapeutic communication

Adapt communication styles to reduce the likelihood of triggering intense rejection reactions.

Explicit positive regard: Be more direct about positive observations and appreciation than you might with neurotypical clients. RSD makes people miss subtle positive cues while amplifying negative ones.

Intention clarification: Explicitly state your positive intentions when offering feedback or suggestions. "I'm bringing this up because I believe in your ability to handle this challenge, not because I think you're doing anything wrong."

Collaborative framing: Frame all suggestions and feedback as collaborative problem-solving rather than expert advice or behavioral correction.

Validation integration: Integrate validation and normalization into all feedback to reduce the likelihood of shame responses.

Choice emphasis: Consistently emphasize the person's autonomy and choice in all recommendations to reduce pressure and control-related triggers.

Preemptive RSD management

Address RSD directly and develop strategies for managing it before it disrupts therapeutic work.

RSD education: Help people understand RSD as a neurological feature rather than emotional weakness, reducing shame about their sensitivity.

Trigger identification: Work together to identify specific types of feedback or interactions that commonly trigger RSD responses.

Signal development: Create agreements about how the person will communicate when they're experiencing RSD so you can adjust your approach immediately.

Recovery strategies: Develop specific techniques for recovering from RSD episodes quickly rather than having them derail entire sessions or therapeutic relationships.

Perspective checking: Build skills for reality-testing RSD interpretations of social interactions against more balanced perspectives.

The therapeutic relationship as healing space

Use the therapeutic relationship itself as an opportunity to provide corrective experiences around rejection and acceptance.

Consistent acceptance: Demonstrate consistent positive regard even when discussing areas of struggle or difficulty.

Mistake normalization: Model that mistakes and imperfections don't result in relationship rupture or withdrawal of support.

Repair practices: When miscommunications occur, demonstrate how to repair relationship ruptures effectively rather than avoiding conflict.

Authentic connection: Show that authentic, imperfect humanity is more valuable than perfect performance in relationships.

Feedback adaptation techniques

Modify how you provide feedback and suggestions to work with RSD sensitivity rather than triggering it.

Sandwich method adaptation: Use genuine positive observations before and after constructive feedback, but ensure the positive elements are authentic rather than manipulative.

Curiosity-based feedback: Frame observations as curious questions rather than definitive statements. "I'm curious about..." rather than "I noticed that you..."

Strength-based reframing: Help people see areas for growth as opportunities to use existing strengths rather than deficits to fix.

Choice-rich suggestions: Offer multiple options rather than single recommendations, emphasizing personal fit and preference.

Timeline flexibility: Remove pressure about timelines and progress expectations that can trigger performance anxiety.

David had severe RSD that made traditional therapy feel threatening and shameful. His therapist adapted by explicitly discussing RSD at the beginning of their work and developing signals David could use when he was feeling criticized or judged. They established a practice of checking in about David's emotional state regularly and adjusting the conversation approach based on his needs. When RSD was activated, they would pause, validate David's experience, and explore what had triggered the response before continuing with therapeutic work. This approach allowed David to engage authentically without constant fear of judgment.

Managing shame and perceived criticism

Shame is often the core emotion underlying RSD responses, and effective therapeutic work requires addressing shame directly rather than trying to work around it. Traditional MI approaches that avoid direct discussion of shame often leave RSD-sensitive individuals feeling misunderstood and disconnected.

Understanding ADHD shame patterns

Shame in ADHD often develops from years of receiving criticism for neurological differences that are often invisible and misunderstood.

Performance-based shame: Repeated experiences of not meeting neurotypical expectations create deep shame about personal adequacy and capability.

Social shame: Difficulties with social communication, executive function, and emotional regulation often lead to shame about being "too much" or "not enough" in relationships.

Productivity shame: Struggles with consistency, follow-through, and traditional productivity measures create shame about being "lazy" or "irresponsible."

Masking exhaustion: The effort required to appear neurotypical is often unsustainable, leading to shame when the mask slips and authentic ADHD traits become visible.

Shame-resilient therapeutic approaches

Build approaches that acknowledge and work with shame rather than inadvertently reinforcing it.

Shame normalization: Help people understand that shame responses are common and understandable given their life experiences with ADHD.

Neurological reframing: Consistently reframe ADHD challenges as neurological differences rather than personal failings or character defects.

Strength integration: Balance discussion of challenges with genuine recognition of ADHD strengths and positive qualities.

Experience validation: Validate the reality of discrimination and misunderstanding that many ADHD individuals have experienced rather than minimizing their social struggles.

Developing shame resilience

Build specific skills for managing shame when it arises rather than trying to avoid it entirely.

Shame recognition: Help people identify early signs of shame responses so they can address them before they become overwhelming.

Self-compassion development: Build practices of treating oneself with the same kindness one would offer a good friend facing similar challenges.

Reality testing skills: Develop abilities to distinguish between accurate self-assessment and shame-based self-criticism.

Support network utilization: Connect with others who understand ADHD and can provide realistic perspective and encouragement.

Contribution focus: Shift attention from personal inadequacies to ways one contributes value to others and the world.

Working with perfectionist patterns

Address perfectionist tendencies that often develop as protection against RSD but ultimately interfere with goal achievement.

Good enough standards: Help people develop realistic standards for "good enough" performance that allow for completion and progress.

Experiment mindset: Reframe goals as experiments rather than pass/fail tests, reducing performance pressure.

Process focus: Emphasize effort and learning process over outcomes to reduce perfectionist pressure.

Mistake reframing: Help people see mistakes as information and learning opportunities rather than evidence of personal inadequacy.

Building resilience while pursuing change

The goal isn't to eliminate RSD or emotional sensitivity but to build resilience that allows for pursuing meaningful goals despite occasional setbacks and interpersonal challenges.

Resilience vs. invulnerability

True resilience involves developing skills for recovering from difficult experiences rather than trying to avoid them entirely.

Bounce-back skills: Focus on developing abilities to recover from rejection, criticism, or setbacks rather than trying to prevent them completely.

Support utilization: Build skills for reaching out for help and connection during difficult periods rather than trying to handle everything alone.

Perspective flexibility: Develop abilities to consider multiple interpretations of social interactions rather than defaulting to rejection assumptions.

Self-soothing capacities: Build repertoire of healthy self-soothing strategies for managing intense emotions when they arise.

Risk-taking in the context of RSD

Help RSD-sensitive individuals develop skills for taking appropriate risks despite fear of rejection or criticism.

Graduated exposure: Start with lower-risk situations that build confidence and skills before tackling higher-risk goals.

Support system preparation: Ensure adequate support systems are in place before attempting challenging goals that might trigger RSD.

Failure planning: Develop specific plans for handling setbacks or criticism that might occur during goal pursuit.

Success recognition: Build skills for recognizing and celebrating progress and success rather than focusing exclusively on areas for improvement.

Long-term resilience development

Build sustainable approaches to emotional regulation that support long-term goal achievement and life satisfaction.

Emotional regulation skills: Develop specific techniques for managing intense emotions without avoiding or suppressing them entirely.

Relationship skills: Build abilities to navigate interpersonal challenges and repair relationship ruptures when they occur.

Self-advocacy development: Develop skills for communicating needs and boundaries in relationships while managing RSD sensitivity.

Identity integration: Build positive identity that integrates both ADHD challenges and strengths rather than focusing exclusively on either.

Community connection: Connect with neurodivergent communities that provide understanding, acceptance, and practical support.

Maria learned to work with her RSD by developing what she called her "rejection recovery kit." When she experienced intense shame or perceived rejection, she had specific steps: first, she would physically comfort herself (weighted blanket, favorite tea); second, she would text a friend who understood ADHD for reality-testing; third, she would write in her journal about the experience; and fourth, she would review her list of personal strengths and recent accomplishments. This system allowed her to recover from RSD episodes quickly and return to pursuing her goals rather than being derailed for days or weeks. Her therapist helped her recognize that having RSD didn't make her weak—it made her human, and humans need good recovery systems.

This completes our exploration of ADHD-specific adaptations to motivational interviewing. The final section of this book will provide practical tools and resources for implementing neurodivergent-adapted MI approaches across different settings and populations.

Creating emotional safety for growth

Rejection Sensitive Dysphoria significantly affects how ADHD individuals experience therapeutic relationships and respond to change-focused conversations. Rather than viewing emotional sensitivity as a barrier to overcome, effective approaches create psychological safety that allows for authentic engagement despite heightened rejection sensitivity.

The key insight is that RSD-sensitive individuals often have tremendous capacity for growth and change when they feel genuinely accepted and supported. This requires adapting traditional MI techniques to minimize shame triggers while building resilience skills that support long-term goal achievement.

Success comes from balancing emotional safety with appropriate challenge, helping people build skills for managing intense emotions while pursuing meaningful changes in their lives.

Chapter 12: Visual MI Tools

Charts, cards, and concrete aids

When Dr. Chen asked 23-year-old Marcus to rate his confidence in completing college on a scale of 1 to 10, he stared at her blankly for several seconds before responding, "I don't know what those numbers mean. Like, is 5 the middle? Is 7 good or bad? How do I translate how I feel into a number?"

Dr. Chen realized that traditional verbal scaling questions weren't connecting with Marcus's way of processing information. She pulled out a visual scale that showed faces ranging from extremely worried to completely confident, with descriptive words under each face. Marcus immediately pointed to the face that showed moderate worry with some hope. "That one. That's exactly how I feel."

This moment changed Dr. Chen's entire approach to motivational interviewing with neurodivergent clients. She discovered that visual tools didn't just make abstract concepts clearer—they made therapeutic conversations more accessible, engaging, and effective for people who think in pictures, patterns, and concrete representations.

Marcus wasn't struggling with self-awareness or motivation. He was struggling with translating his internal experiences into the abstract verbal formats that traditional therapy assumes everyone can use naturally.

Visual scaling and rating tools

Many neurodivergent individuals are visual processors who understand and communicate information more effectively through images, charts, and concrete visual representations than through abstract verbal concepts. Traditional MI scaling questions that ask people to rate things numerically often miss the mark because numbers feel meaningless without visual context.

The limitations of abstract numerical scales

Traditional scaling questions assume that people naturally understand numerical representations of subjective experiences and can accurately translate internal states into numbers.

"On a scale of 1 to 10, how important is this goal to you?"

For many neurodivergent individuals, this question creates several challenges:

Number abstraction difficulty: The relationship between internal experience and numerical ratings isn't intuitive. What's the difference between a 6 and a 7? How do emotions translate to mathematics?

Reference point confusion: Without clear reference points, people might wonder: Is 5 neutral? Is 8 considered high or moderate? What would a 10 feel like?

Processing load: Converting subjective experience into numbers requires executive function and abstract thinking that adds unnecessary cognitive work to the assessment process.

Cultural number meanings: Numbers carry different connotations for different people. Some see 7 as lucky, others as average. These associations can interfere with accurate self-assessment.

Visual alternatives to numerical scales

Replace abstract number scales with visual representations that provide clear, concrete reference points.

Emoji or face scales: Use facial expressions that represent different emotional states or confidence levels. These provide immediate visual recognition of internal experiences.

Color scales: Create scales using color progression (red to yellow to green, or cool to warm colors) that people can connect to their emotional experiences.

Size or intensity scales: Use visual elements that grow larger, brighter, or more intense to represent increasing levels of motivation, confidence, or importance.

Metaphorical visual scales: Create scales based on weather (stormy to sunny), temperature (frozen to boiling), or other visual metaphors that resonate with individual experiences.

Interactive physical scales

Move beyond paper-based tools to create physical, interactive scaling experiences.

Floor scales: Create large floor scales where people can physically position themselves to represent their confidence, motivation, or progress levels.

Object manipulation: Use blocks, cards, or other physical objects that people can arrange to represent their internal states or goals.

Thermometer or gauge tools: Create visual tools that look like thermometers, speedometers, or other familiar measuring devices that people can fill in or point to.

Movement-based scaling: For people who think better while moving, create scales that involve walking, gesturing, or positioning their bodies in space.

Sarah, a 19-year-old autistic college student, struggled with traditional therapy until her counselor introduced visual scaling tools. Instead of asking "How anxious do you feel?" the counselor showed Sarah a visual anxiety thermometer with descriptive labels: "Ice cold calm," "Cool and collected," "Room temperature," "Getting warm," "Hot and bothered," and "Boiling over." Sarah could immediately identify where her anxiety fell on any given day and track changes over time. The visual tool made her internal experiences concrete and shareable in ways that numbers never could.

Customized scaling systems

Work with individuals to create personalized visual scaling systems that align with their interests, thinking patterns, and areas of expertise.

Interest-based scales: Someone passionate about music might use volume controls or musical dynamics (pianissimo to fortissimo) to rate emotional intensity. A sports fan might use scoreboards or performance metrics.

Profession-based scales: A programmer might prefer scales based on system performance (running smoothly, some bugs, major errors, complete crash). An artist might use color saturation or paint consistency metaphors.

Sensory preference scales: Visual processors might prefer image-based scales, while tactile processors might prefer textured materials or physical objects to manipulate.

Personal metaphor scales: Help people identify metaphors that resonate with their experience—energy levels might be represented as battery charge, plant growth, or weather patterns.

Change conversation flowcharts

Many neurodivergent individuals benefit from seeing the structure and flow of therapeutic conversations rather than navigating them purely through verbal interaction. Flowcharts provide visual roadmaps that reduce anxiety about the unknown and help people track where they are in complex discussions.

The cognitive load of unstructured conversation

Open-ended therapeutic conversations can create significant cognitive burden for neurodivergent individuals who benefit from structure and predictability.

Processing uncertainty: Not knowing what topics might come up or how conversations will flow can create anxiety that interferes with authentic engagement.

Working memory demands: Tracking multiple conversation threads, remembering earlier points, and maintaining awareness of overall session goals requires substantial working memory capacity.

Social navigation complexity: Determining when to speak, what to share, how much detail to provide, and how to transition between topics requires social processing that can be exhausting.

Executive function overload: Managing conversation flow while simultaneously processing content and planning responses can overwhelm executive function systems.

Visual conversation maps

Create visual guides that show the structure and flow of motivational interviewing conversations.

Session overview charts: Provide visual outlines showing what will be covered in therapy sessions, how much time each section might take, and what types of activities or discussions to expect.

Decision tree flowcharts: Create flowcharts that show how different responses or insights lead to different conversation directions, helping people understand the logic and flow of MI processes.

Goal progression maps: Visual representations of how change conversations build from initial exploration through goal-setting to action planning, showing the logical progression and interconnections.

Topic relationship diagrams: Visual maps showing how different life areas or goals connect to each other, helping people see patterns and relationships they might miss in purely verbal discussions.

Interactive conversation tools

Create tools that people can manipulate and interact with during conversations rather than just viewing passively.

Moveable topic cards: Create cards representing different topics or life areas that people can physically arrange, prioritize, or group during conversations.

Conversation wheels: Circular tools with different sections representing various aspects of change that people can spin, point to, or use to guide discussion focus.

Build-your-own journey maps: Tools that allow people to create their own visual representation of their change process, adding elements, drawing connections, and modifying the map as insights develop.

Progress tracking boards: Visual boards where people can move markers, add stickers, or otherwise physically represent their progress through change processes.

Reducing conversational anxiety

Use visual conversation tools to reduce anxiety about the therapeutic process and increase engagement.

Agenda transparency: Show people exactly what will be discussed and in what order, reducing anxiety about surprise topics or unexpected directions.

Choice visualization: Present conversation options visually so people can see their choices and make informed decisions about focus and direction.

Progress indicators: Provide visual indicators showing where people are in longer change processes, how much progress they've made, and what steps remain.

Exit strategies: Build visual reminders about how people can take breaks, change topics, or end conversations if they become overwhelming.

Jake, a 16-year-old with ADHD, found therapy sessions confusing and overwhelming until his counselor introduced conversation flowcharts. At the beginning of each session, they would review a simple visual map showing: Check-in (5 minutes), Main topic exploration (20 minutes), Goal-setting or problem-solving (15 minutes), and Wrap-up (5 minutes). Jake could see where they were in the process, how much time remained, and what was coming next. This structure reduced his anxiety and allowed him to engage more fully with the content rather than worrying about the process.

Concrete goal-setting templates

Abstract goal-setting processes can feel overwhelming and meaningless to neurodivergent individuals who think in concrete, specific terms. Visual templates provide structure that makes goal development more accessible and sustainable.

The problems with abstract goal-setting

Traditional goal-setting approaches often rely on abstract thinking and future-focused visualization that doesn't align with concrete thinking patterns.

Vague goal language: Goals like "improve self-care" or "be more social" don't provide enough specific information for concrete thinkers to understand what success looks like or how to take action.

Future-focused abstraction: Imagining hypothetical future states requires abstract thinking that can be challenging for people who think in concrete, present-moment terms.

Overwhelm from complexity: Big, long-term goals can feel so overwhelming that people don't know where to start, leading to procrastination or avoidance.

Lack of concrete success criteria: Without specific, observable criteria for success, it's impossible to know when goals have been achieved or how to track progress.

Visual goal development templates

Create structured templates that guide people through concrete goal development processes.

Goal breakdown charts: Templates that help people break large goals into smaller, specific components with clear action steps and timelines.

SMART goal visual organizers: Charts that guide people through creating Specific, Measurable, Achievable, Relevant, and Time-bound goals with visual prompts and examples.

Before and after comparison tools: Templates that help people visualize their current situation alongside their desired future state, with concrete descriptions of what would be different.

Resource and barrier mapping: Visual tools for identifying what resources are needed to achieve goals and what obstacles might need to be addressed.

Action-oriented visual planning

Focus on concrete actions rather than abstract outcomes, using visual tools to make action planning more engaging and sustainable.

Step-by-step visual guides: Create comic strip-style visual guides showing the specific steps needed to achieve goals, including what each step looks like and how long it might take.

Daily/weekly action calendars: Visual calendars that show exactly when specific goal-related actions will be taken, making abstract intentions concrete and scheduled.

Progress tracking charts: Visual tools for tracking daily or weekly progress toward goals, providing immediate feedback and motivation for continued effort.

Celebration milestone maps: Visual representations of progress milestones with built-in celebration points, making the journey toward goals more rewarding and sustainable.

Collaborative template creation

Work with individuals to create personalized goal-setting templates that align with their thinking patterns, interests, and communication styles.

Individual format preferences: Some people prefer linear lists, others prefer circular or web-based formats, and still others prefer timeline-based visual organizers.

Interest integration: Include elements related to the person's special interests or areas of expertise in goal-setting templates to increase engagement and connection.

Sensory preferences: Create templates that align with sensory preferences—some people prefer colorful, visually rich templates while others prefer simple, high-contrast designs.

Modification flexibility: Build templates that can be easily modified, updated, or completely restructured as goals and circumstances change.

Progress tracking visual aids

Many neurodivergent individuals benefit from immediate, visual feedback about their progress toward goals. Traditional progress tracking through verbal reflection or abstract assessment often doesn't provide the concrete, satisfying evidence of change that sustains motivation over time.

The motivation power of visual progress

Visual progress tracking leverages several psychological principles that are particularly powerful for neurodivergent individuals.

Immediate feedback: Visual progress tools provide immediate evidence of effort and achievement, which is especially important for ADHD brains that need frequent reinforcement.

Concrete evidence: Visual progress tracking makes abstract concepts like "improvement" or "growth" concrete and observable, which aligns with literal thinking patterns.

Pattern recognition: Visual tools allow people to see patterns in their progress over time, identifying what works, what doesn't, and when they tend to make their best progress.

Motivation maintenance: Seeing visual evidence of progress can sustain motivation during difficult periods when internal motivation flags.

Types of visual progress tools

Create different types of visual progress tracking tools to match different goals, personalities, and tracking preferences.

Chart and graph systems: Simple charts that show daily, weekly, or monthly progress toward specific goals with visual elements like colored bars, line graphs, or pictorial representations.

Milestone mapping: Visual representations of major milestones in change processes, with ways to mark completion and celebrate achievements along the journey.

Habit tracking grids: Grid-based systems that allow people to track daily habits or small actions that contribute to larger goals, providing satisfying visual patterns of consistency.

Before-and-after documentation: Visual tools for documenting starting points and regular progress updates through photos, drawings, or other visual evidence of change.

Gamification elements

Incorporate game-like elements into progress tracking to increase engagement and motivation, particularly for individuals who respond well to achievement-based systems.

Point systems: Assign points for different types of goal-related activities, with visual displays of total points accumulated over time.

Badge or achievement systems: Create visual badges or certificates that people earn for reaching specific milestones or maintaining consistent efforts.

Level progression: Design progress tracking systems that use level-up concepts, where people advance through different levels as they make progress toward goals.

Challenge modes: Include optional challenge elements where people can push themselves for extra rewards or recognition while maintaining baseline expectations.

Technology integration options

Leverage technology to create interactive, engaging visual progress tracking systems that work across different devices and contexts.

App-based tracking: Use or recommend smartphone apps that provide visual progress tracking with notifications, reminders, and social sharing options.

Digital photo journals: Systems for taking and organizing photos that document progress over time, particularly useful for goals with visual components.

Online dashboard creation: Web-based tools that allow people to create personalized progress tracking dashboards they can access from anywhere.

Social sharing platforms: For people who benefit from social accountability, platforms that allow sharing progress visually with supportive communities or accountability partners.

Customization and personalization

Work with individuals to create progress tracking systems that match their specific motivation patterns, aesthetic preferences, and goal types.

Visual style preferences: Some people prefer minimalist designs while others enjoy colorful, decorative visual elements. Match the visual style to individual preferences.

Frequency options: Some people benefit from daily tracking while others prefer weekly or monthly check-ins. Build flexibility into tracking systems.

Reward integration: Include personalized reward systems that align with individual interests and motivation patterns.

Modification capabilities: Ensure tracking systems can be easily modified as goals change or as people discover what tracking methods work best for their brains.

Maria, a 35-year-old with autism, wanted to develop better social connections but felt overwhelmed by the abstract nature of "relationship building." Her therapist helped her create a visual goal-setting template that broke social connection into concrete components: "Have one meaningful conversation per week," "Attend one social event per month," "Send two check-in texts to friends per week," and "Join one interest-based group." They created a visual progress chart that looked like a garden, where Maria could add flowers for each goal achievement. Within three months, Maria had a flourishing visual garden that represented real improvements in her social connections, and the concrete tracking system helped her see patterns in what types of social activities worked best for her.

Visual tools in motivational interviewing aren't just helpful additions—they're often essential adaptations that make therapeutic concepts accessible to different thinking styles. When we provide visual, concrete ways to understand scaling, conversation flow, goal-setting, and progress tracking, we open up therapeutic processes to neurodivergent individuals who might otherwise struggle to engage with purely verbal approaches.

The next chapter explores how to adapt the interpersonal dynamics of MI through parallel play approaches that reduce social pressure while maintaining therapeutic connection and effectiveness.

Making abstract concepts concrete

Visual MI tools transform abstract therapeutic concepts into concrete, accessible formats that align with neurodivergent thinking patterns. Rather than forcing people to translate their experiences into verbal abstractions, these tools meet them where their brains naturally function best.

The power of visual tools lies not just in making information clearer but in making therapeutic processes more engaging, less anxiety-provoking, and more effective for individuals who think in pictures, patterns, and concrete representations. When we provide visual scaffolding for scaling, conversation flow, goal-setting, and progress tracking, we often discover remarkable insights and capabilities that remained hidden in traditional verbal-only approaches.

This represents a fundamental shift from asking neurodivergent individuals to adapt to neurotypical therapeutic methods toward adapting therapeutic methods to work with neurodivergent strengths.

Chapter 13: Parallel Play Conversations

Side-by-side MI techniques

Dr. Williams had been struggling to connect with 14-year-old Emma during their therapy sessions. Despite multiple attempts at traditional face-to-face conversation, Emma remained withdrawn, giving minimal responses and avoiding eye contact. The sessions felt stilted and unproductive.

Then one day, Dr. Williams noticed Emma looking longingly at the art supplies on the shelf. On impulse, she suggested they work on a puzzle together while they talked. **Something magical happened when they sat side-by-side, both focused on the puzzle pieces, with conversation flowing naturally around their shared activity.**

Emma began sharing insights about her anxiety, her struggles at school, and her goals for feeling more confident. The same person who had been virtually silent in face-to-face conversation became articulate and reflective when the pressure of direct social interaction was removed.

Dr. Williams discovered that parallel play—engaging in activities alongside each other rather than directly facing each other—could transform therapeutic relationships and make MI conversations accessible to people who struggle with traditional social interaction demands.

Reducing eye contact pressure

For many neurodivergent individuals, sustained eye contact isn't a sign of connection or attention—it's an uncomfortable, distracting, or even painful demand that interferes with their ability to think clearly and communicate effectively. Traditional therapy settings that emphasize face-to-face interaction can inadvertently create barriers to authentic engagement.

Understanding eye contact differences in neurodivergent populations

The neurotypical assumption that eye contact equals attention and respect doesn't hold for many autistic and ADHD individuals.

Autistic eye contact patterns: Many autistic people find direct eye contact overwhelming, distracting, or physically uncomfortable. The effort required to maintain eye contact can interfere with their ability to process conversation content or formulate responses.

ADHD attention patterns: Some individuals with ADHD find that looking away actually helps them focus better on what someone is saying. Visual attention and auditory attention don't always work together optimally.

Cultural and individual variations: Even within neurodivergent populations, preferences for eye contact vary widely. Some people prefer no eye contact, others enjoy brief intermittent contact, and some find certain types of eye contact (brief checking in) more comfortable than sustained gazing.

Processing load considerations: For people who have to consciously manage eye contact rather than doing it automatically, the cognitive effort required can reduce their capacity for the complex thinking required in therapeutic conversations.

Creating low-pressure visual interaction

Adapt the physical setup and social expectations of therapeutic conversations to reduce eye contact pressure while maintaining connection.

Side-by-side seating: Arrange chairs at angles or side-by-side rather than directly facing each other, allowing for natural eye contact when it occurs without making it a constant requirement.

Activity-based focus: Provide activities that create natural focal points other than faces—puzzles, art projects, building activities, or other engaging tasks that allow for conversation while hands and eyes are occupied.

Multiple visual options: Create environments with interesting visual elements (books, artwork, windows, fidget tools) that provide natural places for eyes to rest during conversation.

Explicit permission: Directly communicate that eye contact is not required for meaningful conversation: "Some people focus better when they're looking around the room or working with their hands. Whatever helps you think clearly is fine with me."

Alternative connection indicators

Learn to recognize signs of engagement and connection that don't depend on eye contact.

Body orientation: People who are engaged often orient their bodies toward you even if their eyes are looking elsewhere.

Responsive communication: Active listening, thoughtful questions, and engaged responses indicate connection more reliably than eye contact patterns.

Relaxed posture: When people feel comfortable and connected, their bodies often relax even if they're not making eye contact.

Voluntary sharing: Willingness to share personal information or insights indicates trust and connection regardless of eye contact patterns.

Task engagement: In parallel activities, enthusiastic engagement with shared tasks often indicates comfort and connection.

Accommodating visual processing differences

Recognize that some neurodivergent individuals are highly visual processors who benefit from visual input during conversations while others find visual input distracting.

Visual support tools: For visual processors, include charts, drawings, or other visual aids that provide helpful focal points during conversation.

Visual simplicity: For individuals who find visual input overwhelming, create clean, simple environments with minimal visual distractions.

Movement accommodation: Some people think better when their eyes can scan the environment or track movement, which supports their cognitive processing.

Lighting considerations: Ensure appropriate lighting that works for individual sensory needs—too bright or too dim lighting can interfere with comfort and attention.

Alex, a 22-year-old autistic college student, had avoided therapy for years because the prospect of sitting face-to-face making eye contact felt unbearable. His therapist adapted by suggesting they work on origami together during sessions. With both of their hands busy folding paper and their eyes focused on the shared task, Alex found himself able to discuss his social anxiety, academic struggles, and relationship goals with surprising openness. The parallel activity created a bridge that made intimate conversation feel safe and manageable.

Activity-based conversations

Traditional therapy assumes that people can engage in complex emotional and cognitive processing while sitting still and focusing exclusively on verbal interaction. For many neurodivergent individuals, adding appropriate activities can actually enhance rather than distract from therapeutic engagement.

The cognitive benefits of hands-on activities

Engaging in appropriate activities during therapeutic conversations can support rather than interfere with higher-level thinking and emotional processing.

Cognitive regulation: Many people think more clearly when their hands are busy with simple, repetitive tasks that provide just enough stimulation to optimize attention without overwhelming cognitive resources.

Anxiety reduction: Having something to do with their hands and eyes can reduce social anxiety and self-consciousness, allowing for more authentic communication.

Working memory support: Simple physical activities can actually support working memory by reducing the cognitive load of managing social interaction demands.

Processing time: Activities provide natural pauses and processing time, allowing people to think through responses without the pressure of immediate verbal reaction.

Selecting appropriate therapeutic activities

Choose activities that support rather than compete with conversational engagement.

Simple, repetitive tasks: Activities like folding paper, sorting objects, drawing simple patterns, or working with clay provide gentle stimulation without requiring significant attention.

Familiar, low-skill activities: Choose tasks that people can do easily without having to learn new skills or follow complex instructions during therapy time.

Quiet, non-disruptive options: Select activities that don't create noise or movement that might interfere with conversation or recording if sessions are documented.

Personally meaningful activities: When possible, incorporate activities related to the person's interests or hobbies to increase engagement and comfort.

Collaborative possibilities: Some activities work well for both therapist and client to engage in together, creating shared focus and natural conversation opportunities.

Therapeutic activity categories

Different types of activities serve different therapeutic functions and work better for different individuals.

Art and creative activities: Drawing, coloring, sculpting, or collage work can provide emotional expression opportunities while supporting conversation.

Building and construction: Legos, blocks, or simple craft projects provide satisfying sensory input and problem-solving engagement that supports cognitive function.

Sorting and organizing: Activities like organizing cards, sorting objects by color or size, or working with small manipulatives can be soothing and focusing.

Puzzle and problem-solving: Jigsaw puzzles, word games, or logic puzzles provide just enough cognitive challenge to optimize attention without overwhelming processing capacity.

Nature and sensory activities: Indoor plants, textured materials, or sensory bins can provide calming input that supports emotional regulation during difficult conversations.

Integrating activities with MI techniques

Adapt traditional MI techniques to work naturally with activity-based conversations.

Activity-integrated scaling: "While you're sorting these cards, think about how confident you feel about this goal. Put the cards that represent your confidence level in one pile and the ones that represent your doubts in another."

Creative metaphor development: Use art or building activities to create visual metaphors for goals, challenges, or progress. "What would your ideal life look like if you built it out of these blocks?"

Process reflection through activity: "As you work on this puzzle, I'm curious about how this feels similar to or different from working on your goals in real life."

Collaborative problem-solving: Use shared activities as metaphors for real-life collaboration and problem-solving skills.

Walking meetings and movement integration

Many neurodivergent individuals think more clearly and communicate more effectively when their bodies are in gentle motion. Walking meetings and movement-integrated conversations can dramatically improve therapeutic engagement and effectiveness.

The neuroscience of movement and cognition

Physical movement supports cognitive function through several neurological mechanisms that are particularly relevant for neurodivergent brains.

Executive function enhancement: Gentle physical movement can improve executive function, working memory, and attention regulation through increased blood flow and neurotransmitter activation.

Anxiety reduction: Walking and other rhythmic movements activate the parasympathetic nervous system, reducing anxiety and stress that can interfere with therapeutic engagement.

Dopamine activation: Movement stimulates dopamine production, which is particularly beneficial for ADHD brains that need additional dopamine for optimal cognitive function.

Bilateral brain activation: Walking engages both sides of the brain and can facilitate creative thinking, problem-solving, and insight development.

Sensory regulation: Movement provides vestibular and proprioceptive input that helps many neurodivergent individuals feel more regulated and comfortable in their bodies.

Walking meeting logistics

Create practical systems for incorporating walking into therapeutic conversations.

Route planning: Identify safe, quiet walking routes that provide appropriate privacy for therapeutic conversations. Indoor hallways, outdoor paths, or even pacing in large rooms can work.

Weather considerations: Develop backup plans for inclement weather, such as indoor walking spaces or alternative movement activities.

Safety protocols: Ensure that walking meetings maintain appropriate professional boundaries and safety considerations for both client and therapist.

Duration flexibility: Some people benefit from entire sessions spent walking while others prefer shorter walking segments integrated into seated conversations.

Documentation adaptations: Develop systems for taking notes or documenting sessions that don't require sitting at a desk, such as voice recording or post-session documentation.

Movement variety options

Different types of movement work better for different individuals and different types of therapeutic conversations.

Gentle walking: Slow, steady walking on flat surfaces provides optimal conditions for many people to engage in complex conversation and reflection.

Nature walking: When available, walking in natural settings can provide additional sensory benefits and stress reduction.

Indoor alternatives: Pacing, walking stairs, or moving around large rooms can provide movement benefits when outdoor walking isn't possible.

Desk-based movement: For people who prefer to stay seated, options like rocking chairs, balance balls, or foot pedals can provide gentle movement input.

Standing options: Some people focus better while standing and shifting weight, which can be accommodated with standing desks or high tables.

Conversation pacing for movement

Adapt conversation pacing and structure to work optimally with movement-based interactions.

Natural rhythm matching: Allow conversation to flow with the natural rhythm of walking rather than forcing specific pacing or timing.

Processing breaks: Use walking pace changes or brief stops as natural processing breaks when discussing complex or emotional topics.

Direction changes: Sometimes changing walking direction can provide natural transitions between topics or signal shifts in conversation focus.

Sitting integration: Some conversations benefit from alternating between walking segments and brief sitting periods for more intensive focus or note-taking.

Jordan, a 17-year-old with ADHD, found traditional therapy sessions unbearable because sitting still made him feel restless and unable to concentrate. His therapist began conducting sessions while walking around the school campus. The gentle movement helped Jordan access his thoughts more easily and communicate more authentically about his academic challenges and social goals. The walking conversations became so effective that Jordan actually looked forward to therapy sessions for the first time in his life.

Shared focus approaches

Parallel play principles can be applied to create therapeutic conversations where both participants are focused on shared activities or goals rather than primarily focusing on each other. This reduces social pressure while maintaining meaningful connection and therapeutic progress.

Understanding parallel versus face-to-face interaction

Parallel interaction patterns can feel more natural and sustainable for many neurodivergent individuals than traditional face-to-face social interaction.

Reduced social performance pressure: When focus is on shared activities rather than social interaction itself, people often feel less pressure to perform socially or manage complex social cues.

Natural conversation flow: Conversations that develop around shared tasks or interests often feel more organic and authentic than structured therapeutic dialogues.

Interest-based connection: Parallel activities can incorporate special interests or areas of expertise, allowing people to connect through their strengths and passions.

Comfortable silence: Shared focus activities create natural opportunities for comfortable silence and processing time without social awkwardness.

Collaborative rather than hierarchical: Parallel activities can create more equal, collaborative relationships between therapist and client rather than traditional expert-patient dynamics.

Types of shared focus activities

Choose shared focus activities that provide natural opportunities for meaningful conversation while reducing social interaction demands.

Interest-based projects: Engage in activities related to the person's special interests or hobbies, allowing them to share expertise while working on therapeutic goals.

Learning activities: Explore topics that both participants find interesting, creating opportunities for collaborative discovery and reflection.

Service-oriented projects: Engage in activities that help others or contribute to community, providing shared purpose and natural conversation opportunities.

Problem-solving challenges: Work together on puzzles, games, or other problems that require collaboration and create opportunities for discussing problem-solving approaches.

Creative collaborations: Engage in art, music, writing, or other creative activities that allow for both individual expression and shared creation.

Therapeutic integration in shared focus

Maintain therapeutic goals and MI principles while engaging in parallel activities.

Natural therapeutic moments: Learn to recognize and gently explore therapeutic opportunities that arise naturally during shared activities rather than forcing therapeutic content.

Metaphor development: Help people identify connections between their experience with shared activities and their real-life goals and challenges.

Skill transfer: Explore how strengths and abilities demonstrated in shared activities might apply to other life areas.

Relationship practice: Use shared activities as opportunities to practice communication skills, boundary-setting, and collaborative problem-solving.

Reflection integration: Include natural reflection opportunities about both the shared activity and broader life goals.

Balancing structure and spontaneity

Create enough structure to maintain therapeutic focus while allowing for the spontaneous insights and connections that make parallel play conversations so powerful.

Flexible session planning: Plan activities and potential discussion topics while remaining open to unexpected directions that emerge naturally.

Goal integration: Find ways to connect shared activities to the person's broader therapeutic goals without forcing artificial connections.

Process awareness: Pay attention to how the person engages with shared activities as information about their strengths, challenges, and preferences.

Relationship monitoring: Maintain awareness of the therapeutic relationship and progress even when focus is primarily on shared activities.

Time management: Balance shared focus time with more traditional therapeutic processing to ensure all important topics receive adequate attention.

Kai, a 25-year-old autistic adult, struggled with traditional talk therapy but was passionate about board games. His therapist began incorporating strategy games into their sessions, and they discovered that Kai's approach to games revealed important information about his decision-making patterns, stress responses, and social interaction preferences. Through their shared focus on games, Kai was able to explore his anxiety about social situations, develop problem-solving skills, and practice communication strategies in a context that felt natural and enjoyable to him.

Parallel play approaches in MI create alternatives to traditional face-to-face therapeutic interactions that can be more accessible and effective for many neurodivergent individuals. By reducing eye contact pressure, incorporating activities that support cognitive function, integrating movement, and creating shared focus experiences, we can maintain all the therapeutic benefits of motivational interviewing while adapting the social interaction demands to work with different neurological patterns.

The next chapter explores how to incorporate stimming and movement-based self-regulation into therapeutic settings, recognizing these behaviors as communication and regulation strategies rather than distractions to manage.

Redefining therapeutic connection

Parallel play conversations demonstrate that meaningful therapeutic connection doesn't require traditional face-to-face interaction patterns. By reducing eye contact pressure, incorporating supportive activities, integrating movement, and creating shared focus experiences, we can maintain the collaborative spirit and effectiveness of motivational interviewing while making it accessible to people who struggle with traditional social interaction demands.

The key insight is that authentic engagement and therapeutic progress can occur through side-by-side interaction just as effectively as through direct social interaction—and for many neurodivergent individuals, parallel approaches may be more effective because they reduce social performance pressure while supporting cognitive function.

This represents a fundamental shift from requiring people to adapt to therapeutic methods toward adapting therapeutic methods to honor different social interaction preferences and strengths.

Chapter 14: Stimming and Self-Regulation

Incorporating movement

When 8-year-old Marcus started rocking back and forth during his session with Dr. Patterson, her first instinct was to gently redirect him to sit still. "Marcus, can you try to focus and stop rocking so we can talk?"

Marcus immediately became more agitated, his rocking increased, and he started making small humming sounds. Dr. Patterson interpreted this as defiance or inability to follow directions. **What she didn't understand was that Marcus's rocking wasn't interfering with his ability to focus—it was supporting it.**

The rocking motion helped regulate Marcus's sensory system and gave him the input he needed to feel calm enough to engage in conversation. When Dr. Patterson asked him to stop, she inadvertently removed his primary self-regulation strategy, making it much harder for him to participate in therapy.

The breakthrough came when Dr. Patterson learned to recognize stimming as communication and self-regulation rather than problematic behavior to eliminate. Once she understood that Marcus's movements were serving important neurological functions, she could work with his natural regulation patterns instead of against them.

Understanding stimming as communication and regulation

Stimming (self-stimulatory behavior) is a natural neurological response that serves multiple important functions for neurodivergent individuals. Rather than viewing stimming as disruptive or inappropriate behavior, effective therapeutic approaches recognize it as meaningful communication about internal states and essential self-regulation strategy.

The functions of stimming behavior

Stimming serves several neurological and emotional functions that support overall well-being and cognitive function.

Sensory regulation: Stimming helps regulate sensory input by providing needed stimulation when someone is understimulated or helping process overwhelming sensory information when overstimulated.

Emotional regulation: Repetitive movements and behaviors can help manage intense emotions, providing comfort during stress and helping maintain emotional equilibrium.

Communication of internal states: Different types of stimming often communicate specific internal experiences—excitement, anxiety, boredom, overwhelm, or contentment.

Cognitive support: Many people stim more when thinking deeply or processing complex information, suggesting that stimming supports higher-level cognitive functions.

Self-soothing: Stimming provides comfort and emotional regulation during difficult or overwhelming situations, serving as a healthy coping mechanism.

Common types of stimming behaviors

Stimming behaviors vary widely between individuals but generally fall into several sensory categories.

Visual stimming: Hand-flapping, finger movements in front of eyes, spinning objects, watching repetitive movements, or creating visual patterns.

Auditory stimming: Humming, making vocal sounds, repeating words or phrases, listening to the same music repeatedly, or creating rhythmic sounds.

Tactile stimming: Rubbing textures, squeezing stress balls, picking at skin or clothing, or seeking specific tactile sensations.

Proprioceptive stimming: Rocking, bouncing, spinning, jumping, or other movements that provide body position and movement feedback.

Vestibular stimming: Swinging, spinning, tilting head or body, or other movements that stimulate the balance system.

Oral stimming: Chewing (on appropriate items), sucking, or other oral sensory seeking behaviors.

Stimming versus self-injurious behavior

It's crucial to distinguish between stimming that serves regulatory functions and behaviors that cause harm or distress.

Helpful stimming: Behaviors that provide regulation, comfort, or communication without causing physical harm or significant social disruption.

Concerning behaviors: Self-injurious behaviors that cause physical harm, or stimming that creates significant distress for the individual or severely impacts their ability to participate in important activities.

Context considerations: The same behavior might be helpful in some contexts (private time, stress relief) but problematic in others (during important activities, in unsafe situations).

Individual assessment: Work with each person to understand what their specific stimming behaviors communicate and how they function in different contexts.

Stimming as neurological diversity

Research increasingly shows that stimming is a natural feature of neurodivergent neurology rather than a problem to fix (Kapp et al., 2019).

Neurotypical stimming: Even neurotypical individuals engage in stimming behaviors (foot tapping, hair twirling, pen clicking) but these are often more socially accepted.

Intensity differences: Neurodivergent individuals often need more intense or frequent stimming to achieve the same regulatory benefits that neurotypical people get from subtle movements.

Sensory processing connections: Stimming patterns often correlate with individual sensory processing profiles and can provide important information about sensory needs.

Identity and authenticity: For many neurodivergent individuals, stimming is an important part of their authentic self-expression and emotional regulation system.

Supporting self-regulation during conversations

Rather than suppressing stimming during therapeutic conversations, effective approaches support and accommodate self-regulation needs while maintaining focus on therapeutic goals.

Creating stim-friendly therapeutic environments

Design therapeutic spaces that support rather than suppress natural self-regulation behaviors.

Stimming tool availability: Keep appropriate fidget tools, textured objects, stress balls, or other stimming supports readily available during sessions.

Movement accommodation: Arrange spaces to allow for natural movement—rocking chairs, standing options, or space for pacing or position changes.

Sensory considerations: Ensure lighting, sound, and other environmental factors support rather than interfere with sensory regulation needs.

Privacy and acceptance: Create environments where people feel safe to stim naturally without judgment or social pressure to suppress their regulatory behaviors.

Recognizing stimming communication

Learn to interpret different types of stimming as information about the person's internal state and therapeutic needs.

Stress indicators: Increased stimming often signals rising stress, overwhelm, or anxiety, suggesting a need to adjust conversation pace or intensity.

Engagement patterns: Some people stim more when deeply engaged with interesting topics, while others stim more when bored or understimulated.

Processing signals: Changes in stimming patterns might indicate that someone is processing complex information and needs more time to think.

Comfort levels: Relaxed, gentle stimming often indicates comfort and emotional safety, while tense or agitated stimming might signal distress.

Collaborative stimming accommodation

Work with individuals to understand their specific stimming needs and develop appropriate accommodations.

Stimming assessment: "I notice you rock back and forth sometimes. Does that help you think or feel better? What other movements or activities help you feel comfortable and focused?"

Accommodation planning: "What would help you feel most comfortable during our conversations? Are there movements or fidget tools that support your thinking?"

Boundary setting: "Are there any movements or stimming behaviors that feel private to you, or are you comfortable stimming however feels natural during our sessions?"

160

Environment adaptation: "How can we set up this space to work best for your body and brain? What changes would help you feel more comfortable?"

Stimming integration in MI techniques

Adapt traditional MI techniques to work with rather than against natural stimming patterns.

Movement-based scaling: "While you're rocking, think about how motivated you feel about this goal. Rock faster if you feel more motivated, slower if you feel less motivated."

Fidget-supported reflection: Provide fidget tools during reflection exercises, recognizing that hand movement often supports rather than interferes with deep thinking.

Stimming rhythm pacing: Allow conversation pacing to flow with natural stimming rhythms rather than forcing artificial timing that disrupts regulatory patterns.

Energy matching: When someone's stimming indicates high energy or excitement, match that energy in your therapeutic response rather than trying to calm them down.

Lily, a 12-year-old autistic girl, hand-flapped when excited and rocked when anxious. Instead of asking her to stop these behaviors, her therapist learned to recognize them as valuable information. When Lily hand-flapped while discussing her interest in marine biology, the therapist knew this was a high-engagement topic they could use to build motivation for other goals. When Lily rocked more intensely, the therapist knew to slow down, provide reassurance, or shift to less overwhelming topics. By working with Lily's stimming rather than against it, therapy became much more effective and comfortable for both of them.

Movement breaks and sensory tools

Many neurodivergent individuals need regular movement breaks and sensory input to maintain optimal functioning during

therapeutic conversations. Rather than viewing these as interruptions to therapy, successful approaches integrate movement and sensory support as essential elements of effective therapeutic engagement.

The necessity of movement breaks

Extended periods of sitting and talking can be neurologically difficult for many neurodivergent individuals, requiring regular breaks to maintain attention and emotional regulation.

Attention regulation: Movement breaks help reset attention systems and prevent the cognitive fatigue that comes from sustained focus demands.

Sensory reset: Breaks provide opportunities to address sensory needs that might be building up during conversation—too much or too little stimulation, uncomfortable body positions, or environmental factors.

Emotional regulation: Movement and sensory breaks can help process intense emotions that arise during therapeutic conversations, preventing overwhelm.

Executive function support: Regular breaks reduce the executive function demands of sustained conversation and complex thinking.

Types of therapeutic movement breaks

Different types of movement breaks serve different regulatory functions and work better for different individuals.

Active movement breaks: Walking, stretching, jumping, or other physically active breaks that provide vestibular and proprioceptive input.

Calming movement breaks: Gentle rocking, slow stretching, or other soothing movements that help regulate arousal levels downward.

Sensory breaks: Opportunities to address specific sensory needs—dim lighting for visual breaks, noise-canceling headphones for auditory breaks, or textured materials for tactile input.

Transition breaks: Brief pauses between topics that allow for mental gear-shifting and preparation for new content.

Choice-driven breaks: Allowing individuals to choose when they need breaks and what type of break would be most helpful.

Sensory tool integration

Provide appropriate sensory tools that support regulation during therapeutic conversations without becoming distracting.

Tactile tools: Stress balls, thinking putty, textured fabric strips, or fidget cubes that provide hand stimulation during conversation.

Proprioceptive tools: Weighted lap pads, compression vests, or other tools that provide deep pressure input for body awareness and calming.

Vestibular tools: Rocking chairs, balance balls, or other seating options that provide gentle movement input.

Auditory tools: Noise-canceling headphones, white noise machines, or soft background music to support auditory processing needs.

Visual tools: Sunglasses for light sensitivity, visual schedules for predictability, or calming visual focal points.

Creating sensory tool protocols

Develop clear, collaborative protocols for how sensory tools will be used during therapeutic sessions.

Tool introduction: "I have various tools available that some people find helpful for focusing or feeling comfortable. Would you like to try any of these, or do you have tools that work well for you?"

Usage guidelines: Establish guidelines about when and how tools can be used—some people need them constantly, others prefer them only during difficult topics.

Personal tool policies: Many people have specific tools that work best for their sensory needs. Develop policies about bringing personal fidget tools or sensory supports.

Tool maintenance: Ensure sensory tools are clean, safe, and in good working condition, and have backup options available.

Timing movement and sensory breaks

Develop sensitivity to when movement and sensory breaks are needed rather than forcing predetermined break schedules.

Individual signal recognition: Learn to recognize each person's specific signs that they need movement or sensory input.

Proactive break offering: Offer breaks before people become overwhelmed rather than waiting for distress signals.

Flexible break timing: Allow breaks to occur naturally in conversation rather than only at predetermined times.

Break integration: Build movement and sensory input into therapeutic activities rather than treating breaks as interruptions to therapy.

Recognizing overstimulation and dysregulation signs

Learning to recognize early signs of sensory overload and emotional dysregulation allows for proactive intervention that prevents therapeutic conversations from becoming overwhelming or counterproductive.

Early warning signs of overstimulation

Overstimulation often builds gradually, and early recognition allows for intervention before it becomes overwhelming.

Changes in stimming patterns: Increased intensity, frequency, or agitation in stimming behaviors often signals rising stress or sensory overload.

Communication changes: Shorter responses, difficulty finding words, repetitive phrases, or reduced verbal communication can indicate processing overwhelm.

Physical signs: Changes in posture, increased muscle tension, fidgeting, restlessness, or physical signs of stress.

Attention changes: Difficulty maintaining focus, increased distractibility, or seeming "checked out" can indicate overwhelm.

Emotional reactivity: Increased irritability, emotional intensity, or reactions that seem disproportionate to the situation.

Sensory overload indicators

Different types of sensory overload present with different patterns of behavior and distress.

Auditory overload: Covering ears, asking for quiet, seeming startled by normal sounds, or difficulty processing verbal information.

Visual overload: Squinting, looking away, covering eyes, or reporting that lights or visual stimuli feel overwhelming.

Tactile overload: Avoiding touch, pulling away from textures, or seeming uncomfortable with clothing or seating.

Vestibular overload: Dizziness, nausea, or discomfort with movement or position changes.

Proprioceptive seeking: Increased need for deep pressure, movement, or body awareness input.

Dysregulation response strategies

When overstimulation or dysregulation occurs, respond with support and accommodation rather than pushing through or ignoring the signs.

Immediate environmental modifications: Adjust lighting, reduce noise, provide space, or modify other environmental factors that might be contributing to overload.

Regulation support: Offer appropriate sensory tools, movement opportunities, or other regulation strategies that help restore optimal functioning.

Pacing adjustments: Slow down conversation, reduce complexity, or shift to less demanding topics until regulation is restored.

Choice and control: Offer options about how to proceed—continue with modifications, take a longer break, or reschedule if needed.

Validation and normalization: Acknowledge that overstimulation is a normal neurological response rather than a personal failing or therapeutic resistance.

Recovery and prevention planning

Work collaboratively to develop strategies for both recovering from dysregulation and preventing future episodes.

Recovery protocols: Develop personalized strategies for returning to optimal functioning after overstimulation or emotional dysregulation.

Prevention planning: Identify environmental modifications, pacing changes, or other adaptations that reduce the likelihood of overload.

Communication systems: Establish ways for people to communicate their regulation needs before reaching crisis points.

Self-advocacy development: Build skills for recognizing internal states and communicating needs proactively.

Environmental control: Increase individual control over environmental factors that affect regulation—seating, lighting, sound, breaks, etc.

Ben, a 19-year-old with autism, would shut down completely when he became overstimulated during therapy sessions. His therapist learned to recognize the early signs—Ben's speech would become more formal and scripted, his stimming would decrease (indicating he was using energy to suppress it), and he would start giving very brief answers. When the therapist noticed these signs, they would immediately offer a sensory break with Ben's weighted blanket and noise-canceling headphones. After 10-15 minutes of regulation support, Ben could usually re-engage with the conversation. This proactive approach prevented the complete shutdowns that had previously derailed entire sessions.

Understanding stimming and self-regulation as essential neurological functions rather than behaviors to manage transforms therapeutic relationships. When we support natural regulation strategies and recognize signs of dysregulation, we create conditions where neurodivergent individuals can bring their best functioning to therapeutic conversations.

The final chapter explores how to use these neurodivergent-adapted MI approaches to build self-advocacy skills that enable individuals to communicate their needs and manage their own accommodation requirements across different life contexts.

Supporting natural regulation

Stimming and self-regulation behaviors are neurological necessities rather than problems to eliminate. When therapeutic approaches support natural regulation strategies, provide appropriate sensory tools, incorporate movement breaks, and respond skillfully to overstimulation, neurodivergent individuals can engage more authentically and effectively in change conversations.

The paradigm shift is from viewing stimming as disruptive behavior toward recognizing it as valuable communication about internal states and essential self-regulation strategy. This creates therapeutic environments where people can bring their whole, authentic selves to the change process rather than having to suppress important aspects of their neurological functioning.

This approach often reveals remarkable therapeutic engagement and insight that remained hidden when people had to use their energy managing social expectations rather than focusing on personal growth.

Chapter 15: Neurodivergent Self-Advocacy

Building self-awareness

Twenty-six-year-old Rachel had spent most of her life accommodating other people's expectations and trying to appear "normal." She had completed college, landed a good job, and maintained friendships, but she felt exhausted all the time. When she received her ADHD diagnosis at age 25, she felt relief and confusion in equal measure.

"I spent so much energy trying to be someone I'm not," she told her therapist. "But now I don't know how to be myself. I don't even know what I actually need versus what I think I should need."

Rachel's situation illustrates one of the most important goals of neurodivergent-adapted motivational interviewing: building self-advocacy skills that enable people to understand their own needs, communicate them effectively, and create environments that support their authentic functioning.

The journey from external accommodation to internal self-awareness and advocacy represents a fundamental shift from surviving in neurotypical systems to thriving as a neurodivergent individual.

Developing personal accommodation awareness

Many neurodivergent individuals have spent years adapting themselves to environments and expectations that don't match their neurological needs. Developing self-advocacy skills begins with understanding their own accommodation requirements and recognizing these as legitimate needs rather than personal weaknesses or excessive demands.

From masking to authentic needs assessment

Masking—the process of suppressing neurodivergent traits to appear neurotypical—often disconnects people from awareness of their actual needs and preferences.

Masking awareness: Help people recognize the difference between their authentic neurological needs and the behaviors they've developed to appear socially acceptable.

Energy cost recognition: Many accommodations that neurodivergent individuals need aren't luxuries—they're energy conservation strategies that prevent burnout and support sustainable functioning.

Unmasking process: The process of reducing masking behaviors and expressing authentic needs often requires significant support and practice in safe environments.

Identity integration: Developing self-advocacy requires integrating neurodivergent identity as a positive aspect of self rather than something to hide or overcome.

Comprehensive needs assessment

Work with individuals to identify their specific accommodation needs across different life domains.

Sensory accommodation needs: What environmental modifications support optimal functioning? Lighting, sound, texture, temperature, and spatial considerations.

Communication accommodation needs: How do they communicate most effectively? Processing time, written versus verbal communication, direct versus indirect communication styles.

Social accommodation needs: What types of social interaction and what social environments work best? Group size preferences, interaction styles, social energy management.

170

Executive function support needs: What external supports help with planning, organization, time management, and task completion?

Learning and processing accommodation needs: How do they learn and process information most effectively? Visual, auditory, kinesthetic, or multimodal preferences.

Distinguishing needs from wants

Help people differentiate between essential accommodations that support basic functioning and preferences that enhance comfort but aren't strictly necessary.

Survival accommodations: Basic environmental and social modifications that are necessary for sustainable functioning and mental health.

Optimization accommodations: Modifications that significantly improve performance, comfort, or quality of life but aren't essential for basic functioning.

Preference accommodations: Changes that are enjoyable and beneficial but can be adapted or modified based on circumstances.

Context-dependent needs: Some accommodations might be essential in certain contexts (work, school) but less important in others (casual social situations).

Personal accommodation inventory

Create systematic approaches for identifying and documenting individual accommodation needs.

Environmental assessment: Review different environments where the person spends time and identify what works well and what creates challenges.

Activity analysis: Examine different types of activities and identify which are naturally engaging versus which require significant effort or accommodation.

Energy tracking: Monitor energy levels throughout different activities and environments to identify what supports versus drains energy.

Success pattern analysis: Look at times when the person has been successful and identify what environmental or social factors contributed to that success.

Stress pattern identification: Examine situations that reliably create stress or difficulty and identify what modifications might help.

Maya, a 24-year-old autistic graduate student, had always struggled in traditional classrooms but didn't understand why until she began systematically assessing her needs. She discovered that fluorescent lighting gave her headaches, background noise made it impossible to concentrate, and sitting in chairs for long periods caused physical discomfort that interfered with learning. Once she identified these specific needs, she was able to request classroom accommodations that transformed her academic experience: sitting in the back near a window, using a cushion for seating comfort, and permission to step outside for brief breaks when needed.

Communication about needs and preferences

Once neurodivergent individuals develop awareness of their accommodation needs, the next challenge is learning to communicate these needs effectively to others in ways that increase understanding and cooperation.

Overcoming accommodation shame

Many neurodivergent individuals experience shame about their accommodation needs, viewing them as evidence of personal inadequacy rather than neurological differences that require environmental support.

Reframing accommodations: Help people understand accommodations as accessibility needs similar to ramps for wheelchair users rather than special treatment or personal failing.

Medical model versus social model: Explore the difference between viewing neurodivergence as individual pathology versus societal barriers that can be addressed through reasonable accommodations.

Strengths integration: Connect accommodation needs to strengths and positive qualities rather than focusing exclusively on challenges or deficits.

Community normalization: Connect with other neurodivergent individuals who model healthy self-advocacy to normalize accommodation requests.

Clear communication strategies

Develop specific skills for explaining accommodation needs in ways that increase understanding and compliance.

Concrete explanations: Use specific, concrete language to explain needs rather than abstract concepts that might be misunderstood.

Instead of: "I need a quiet environment because I'm sensitive." Try: "Background noise makes it difficult for me to process information accurately. Could we meet in a quieter room or provide noise-canceling headphones?"

Function-based explanations: Explain how accommodations support performance rather than focusing on personal comfort or preference.

Instead of: "Bright lights bother me." Try: "Fluorescent lighting causes headaches that interfere with my ability to concentrate. Using desk lamps instead would help me maintain focus during our meetings."

Benefit framing: Explain how accommodations benefit not just the individual but also the broader goals of the situation.

"When I can fidget with a stress ball during meetings, I'm able to maintain better focus and contribute more effectively to our discussions."

Timing and context considerations

Learn strategic approaches for when and how to request accommodations in different situations.

Proactive versus reactive timing: Request accommodations before problems arise rather than waiting until difficulties have already impacted performance.

Appropriate contexts: Identify which accommodations can be requested formally through official channels versus which might be addressed through informal communication.

Relationship building: Develop positive relationships before requesting accommodations when possible, creating foundation of trust and goodwill.

Documentation preparation: For formal accommodation requests, prepare appropriate documentation and understand relevant laws and policies.

Handling resistance and questions

Develop skills for responding to resistance, skepticism, or invasive questions about accommodation needs.

Boundary setting: Learn to distinguish between appropriate clarifying questions and inappropriate demands for personal medical information.

Education balance: Decide how much education about neurodivergence to provide versus when to simply assert accommodation rights.

Alternative solutions: When specific accommodations aren't possible, negotiate alternative approaches that meet the same functional needs.

Support system activation: Know when and how to involve disability services offices, HR departments, or other institutional support systems.

Self-advocacy skill building through MI

Motivational interviewing principles and techniques can be applied to help neurodivergent individuals develop stronger self-advocacy skills and build confidence in asserting their needs.

Building advocacy motivation

Help people develop internal motivation for self-advocacy by exploring the costs of not advocating and the benefits of effective self-advocacy.

Current cost assessment: "What happens in your life when your accommodation needs aren't met? How does this affect your energy, performance, and well-being?"

Advocacy benefits exploration: "What would be different in your life if you could consistently get the accommodations you need? How would that impact your daily experience?"

Values connection: "How does advocating for your needs align with your values? What's important to you about being authentic versus accommodating others' expectations?"

Future vision: "What would your ideal work/school/living situation look like if all your accommodation needs were met?"

Confidence building strategies

Use MI techniques to build confidence in self-advocacy abilities and overcome fears about requesting accommodations.

Success identification: "Tell me about a time when you successfully asked for something you needed. What made that possible? What strengths did you use?"

Gradual exposure planning: "What would be a small, low-risk way to practice asking for accommodations? Where do you feel safest starting this process?"

Skill recognition: "What communication skills do you already have that could apply to self-advocacy? How are you already effective in other areas of communication?"

Support system identification: "Who in your life supports your authentic self? Who could help you practice or provide backup when you need to advocate for accommodations?"

Role-playing and practice

Provide safe opportunities to practice self-advocacy conversations and develop confidence in different scenarios.

Accommodation request practice: Role-play different scenarios for requesting accommodations in work, school, or social contexts.

Response preparation: Practice responses to common questions, resistance, or challenges that might arise during accommodation requests.

Assertiveness skill development: Build skills for being direct and clear while maintaining appropriate relationships and professionalism.

Conflict resolution practice: Develop skills for handling situations where accommodation requests are denied or met with resistance.

Building advocacy persistence

Help people develop resilience and persistence for self-advocacy, recognizing that it's often an ongoing process rather than one-time requests.

Long-term perspective: "Self-advocacy is a skill that develops over time. How can you approach this as a learning process rather than expecting immediate perfection?"

Setback recovery: "When accommodation requests don't go as hoped, how can you learn from the experience and try again rather than giving up?"

System navigation: "Different systems (work, school, healthcare) have different processes for accommodations. How can you learn to work effectively within different systems?"

Community building: "How can you connect with other people who understand self-advocacy challenges and can provide support and advice?"

Transitioning to independent change management

The ultimate goal of neurodivergent-adapted MI is helping individuals develop skills for managing their own change processes and accommodation needs without requiring ongoing professional support.

Internalized MI skills

Help people develop internal versions of MI techniques they can use for their own goal-setting and change management.

Self-reflection skills: "How can you check in with yourself regularly about what's working and what isn't in your life? What questions can you ask yourself?"

Personal goal-setting: "What process works best for you when setting and pursuing personal goals? How can you break down complex changes into manageable steps?"

Motivation maintenance: "What helps you stay motivated when working toward goals? How can you provide yourself with the encouragement and support you need?"

Obstacle problem-solving: "When you encounter barriers to your goals, what process can you use to figure out solutions or modifications?"

Self-monitoring and adjustment systems

Develop personalized systems for monitoring accommodation effectiveness and making adjustments as needed.

Regular needs assessment: "How often should you reassess your accommodation needs? What changes in your life might require different accommodations?"

Effectiveness tracking: "How will you know if your accommodations are working well? What signs indicate that modifications might be needed?"

Environmental scanning: "As you move into new environments or situations, what process will help you identify your needs and make appropriate requests?"

Feedback integration: "How can you use feedback from others to improve your self-advocacy without compromising your authentic needs?"

Building support networks

Help people develop ongoing support systems that provide encouragement, feedback, and practical assistance with self-advocacy.

Peer support identification: "Who are people in your life who understand and support your neurodivergence? How can you stay connected with them?"

Professional support planning: "What types of professional support (therapy, coaching, disability services) do you want to maintain? How will you know when you need additional support?"

Mentor relationship development: "Are there other neurodivergent individuals who model effective self-advocacy? How might you learn from their experiences?"

Community involvement: "How can you stay connected with neurodivergent communities that provide understanding, resources, and mutual support?"

Preparing for life transitions

Help people develop skills for managing self-advocacy needs during major life transitions when accommodation requirements might change.

Transition preparation: "When you start new jobs, schools, or living situations, what process will help you assess and communicate your needs effectively?"

Documentation systems: "How will you maintain records of effective accommodations so you can communicate about them in new situations?"

Rights and resources awareness: "How will you stay informed about your rights and available resources in different contexts (legal protections, disability services, advocacy organizations)?"

Flexible adaptation: "How can you adapt your self-advocacy approach for different contexts while maintaining your core needs and authentic self?"

David, a 29-year-old with both ADHD and autism, worked with his therapist to develop comprehensive self-advocacy skills. They started by identifying his specific needs across different life domains, then practiced communicating these needs in various contexts. David learned to request accommodations proactively rather than waiting until he was overwhelmed, and he developed confidence in explaining how his accommodations benefited both his performance and the broader goals of his workplace. Over time, David became skilled at assessing new environments, identifying his needs, and advocating effectively for appropriate accommodations. Most importantly, he developed a strong sense of his own worth and the legitimacy of his accommodation needs, transforming from someone who apologized for his differences to someone who confidently advocated for his neurological needs.

Building self-advocacy skills represents the culmination of neurodivergent-adapted motivational interviewing. When people develop clear awareness of their needs, skills for communicating these needs effectively, and confidence in their right to accommodation, they become empowered to create environments that support their authentic functioning and personal goals.

This transformation from external accommodation to internal advocacy represents the ultimate success of neurodivergent-adapted MI: individuals who can navigate the world authentically while advocating effectively for the conditions they need to thrive.

Empowering authentic living

Self-advocacy development represents the transformation from adapting oneself to unsuitable environments toward creating environments that support authentic neurodivergent functioning. Through developing accommodation awareness, communication skills, advocacy confidence, and independent change management abilities, neurodivergent individuals can move from surviving to thriving.

The journey from masking and accommodation to self-advocacy and authenticity is perhaps the most important outcome of neurodivergent-adapted motivational interviewing. When people develop these skills, they gain the ability to create the conditions they need for success across all areas of life.

This represents the ultimate goal: neurodivergent individuals who understand their needs, communicate them effectively, and advocate confidently for the accommodations that enable them to contribute their unique strengths and perspectives to the world.

Final Reflections

This comprehensive guide to neurodivergent-adapted motivational interviewing represents a fundamental shift in how we approach therapeutic conversations with autistic and ADHD individuals. Rather than expecting neurodivergent people to adapt themselves to neurotypical therapeutic methods, these approaches adapt therapeutic methods to honor and work with neurodivergent strengths and needs.

The techniques and perspectives presented throughout these chapters aren't just helpful additions to traditional MI—they're essential adaptations that make therapeutic change processes accessible to individuals whose brains work differently. When we create sensory-friendly environments, use concrete language, leverage special interests, provide visual tools, reduce social pressure, support natural regulation strategies, and build self-advocacy skills, we often discover remarkable capabilities and insights that remained hidden in traditional approaches.

The ultimate goal is enabling neurodivergent individuals to pursue meaningful change while honoring their authentic neurological reality—creating a world where different brains are supported to thrive rather than forced to conform.

Reference

American Psychiatric Association. (2013). *Diagnostic and statistical manual of mental disorders* (5th ed.). American Psychiatric Publishing.

Barkley, R. A. (Ed.). (2014). *Attention-deficit hyperactivity disorder: A handbook for diagnosis and treatment* (4th ed.). Guilford Press.

Ben-Sasson, A., Hen, L., Fluss, R., Cermak, S. A., Engel-Yeger, B., & Gal, E. (2009). A meta-analysis of sensory modulation symptoms in individuals with autism spectrum disorders. *Journal of Autism and Developmental Disorders, 39*(1), 1–11. https://doi.org/10.1007/s10803-008-0593-3

Charlop-Christy, M. H., & Haymes, L. K. (1996). Using obsessions as reinforcers with and without mild reductive procedures to decrease inappropriate behaviors of children with autism. *Journal of Autism and Developmental Disorders, 26*(5), 527–546. https://doi.org/10.1007/BF02172274

Crompton, C. J., Ropar, D., Evans-Williams, C. V. M., Flynn, E. G., & Fletcher-Watson, S. (2020). Autistic peer-to-peer information transfer is highly effective. *Autism, 24*(7), 1704–1712. https://doi.org/10.1177/1362361320919286.

Dodson, W. (2020). Rejection sensitive dysphoria: How to treat this common ADHD condition. *ADDitude Magazine.* https://www.additudemag.com/rejection-sensitive-dysphoria-and-adhd/

Flower, R. L., Benn, R., Bury, S., Camin, M., Muggleton, J., Richardson, E. K., ... Jellett, R. (2025). Defining neurodiversity affirming psychology practice for autistic adults: A Delphi study integrating psychologist and client perspectives. *Autism in Adulthood.* Advance online publication. https://doi.org/10.1089/aut.2024.0305.

Hartanto, T. A., Krafft, C. E., Iosif, A. M., & Schweitzer, J. B. (2016). A trial-by-trial analysis reveals more intense physical activity is associated with better cognitive control performance in attention-deficit/hyperactivity disorder. *Child Neuropsychology, 22*(5), 618–626. https://doi.org/10.1080/09297049.2015.1044511

Kapp, S. K., Steward, R., Crane, L., Elliott, D., Elphick, C., Pellicano, E., & Russell, G. (2019). 'People should be allowed to do what they like': Autistic adults' views and experiences of stimming. *Autism, 23*(7), 1782–1792. https://doi.org/10.1177/1362361319829628

Kasper, L. J., Alderson, R. M., & Hudec, K. L. (2012). Moderators of working memory deficits in children with attention-deficit/hyperactivity disorder (ADHD): A meta-analytic review. *Clinical Psychology Review, 32*(7), 605–617. https://doi.org/10.1016/j.cpr.2012.07.001

Kinnaird, E., Stewart, C., & Tchanturia, K. (2019). Investigating alexithymia in autism: A systematic review and meta-analysis. *European Psychiatry, 55*, 80–89. https://doi.org/10.1016/j.eurpsy.2018.09.004

Kofler, M. J., Sarver, D. E., & Wells, E. L. (2020). Working memory and increased activity level (hyperactivity) in ADHD: Experimental evidence for a functional relation. *Journal of Attention Disorders, 24*(9), 1330–1344. https://doi.org/10.1177/1087054715608439. (SAGE Journals, discovery.fiu.edu)

Milton, D. E. M. (2012). On the ontological status of autism: The "double empathy problem." *Disability & Society, 27*(6), 883–887. https://doi.org/10.1080/09687599.2012.710008

Ne'eman, A. (2010). The future (and the past) of autism advocacy, or why the ASA's magazine, *The Advocate,* wouldn't publish this piece. *Disability Studies Quarterly, 30*(1). https://doi.org/10.18061/dsq.v30i1.1059

Sarver, D. E., Rapport, M. D., Kofler, M. J., Raiker, J. S., & Friedman, L. M. (2015). Hyperactivity in attention-deficit/hyperactivity disorder (ADHD): Impairing deficit or compensatory behavior? *Journal of Abnormal Child Psychology, 43*(7), 1219–1232. https://doi.org/10.1007/s10802-015-0011-1

Söderlund, G. B. W., Sikström, S., & Smart, A. (2007). Listen to the noise: Noise is beneficial for cognitive performance in ADHD. *Journal of Child Psychology and Psychiatry, 48*(8), 840–847. https://doi.org/10.1111/j.1469-7610.2007.01749.x.

Volkow, N. D., Wang, G.-J., Kollins, S. H., Wigal, T. L., Newcorn, J. H., Telang, F., … & Swanson, J. M. (2009). Evaluating dopamine reward pathway in ADHD: Clinical implications. *JAMA, 302*(10), 1084–1091. https://doi.org/10.1001/jama.2009.1308

Printed in Poland
by Amazon Fulfillment
Poland Sp. z o.o., Wrocław

61985393R00103